The Rape

The Rape of Britain

Colin Amery and Dan Cruickshank

Foreword by Sir John Betjeman

Paul Elek London

The illustration opposite the title page shows the outline of
Dance's Circus amid the blazing ruins of its remains, with
the Royal Mint in the background. City of London.

The illustration on the cover is the view from a turning off
Lower Stone Street, Maidstone.

First published 1975 in Great Britain by

Elek Books Limited,
54-58 Caledonian Road,
London N1 9RN.

ISBN 0 236 30943 9 cased
     0 236 31019 4 limp board

Printed and bound in Great Britain by
Unwin Brothers Limited,
The Gresham Press, Old Woking, Surrey

A member of the Staples Printing Group

Contents

Acknowledgments

The authors would like to express their grateful appreciation for the help given to them in the preparation of this book by the following: Oliver Barrett, the Cockburn Association; the Bath Preservation Trust; the Berwick Preservation Trust; Dorothy Brown; Peter Coard; Mrs Dance, the Society for the Protection of Ancient Buildings; the staff of the Department of the Environment; Jane Fawcett, the Victorian Society; Adam Fergusson; Stephen Fry, the Soho Society; Anthony Goodall; Stuart Haden; Laura Hicks, Librarian, the Civic Trust; Ken Lee; the Lincoln Society; David Lloyd; Andy Macmillan; J. D. Macmillan; Michael Millward, the Wisbech Society; Dickon Robinson; John Schofield; Dick Swain. The authors of course take full responsibility for any errors of fact, and the opinions they express are their own.

All the pictures were taken by Dan Cruickshank with the exception of the following: opposite title page John Chesshyre; Introduction, p. 9 top Bath Reference Library; Berwick, 3 Gordon Miller; Cardiff Martin Meade; Cheltenham Anina Hutton; Edinburgh, 15 Anthony Blackley; Hereford, 2, 3, 5, 8, 9, 10 Anina Hutton; Holywell Martin Meade; Hull, 1, 3 Dick Swain; King's Lynn Anina Hutton; Wisbech, 2 Wisbech Museum; Ashford, 1 Weavers, Ashford, Kent, 2-5 *Kentish Express;* And...: Canterbury John Chesshyre; Cockermouth National Monuments Record; Devizes Simon Rogers; Didcot Martin Robertson; Exeter Martin Robertson; Scarborough John Hall.

The following pictures are the copyright of the Architectural Press: Introduction, p. 9 bottom; Bath 1, 3, 4, 5, 7, 8, 9, 10, 11; Berwick 1, 2, 4, 5, 7, 8, 9; Chesterfield 1, 2, 3, 5; Edinburgh 1, 2, 3, 4, 5, 6, 7, 8, 9, 10, 11, 12, 13, 14; Frome 1, 2, 3, 4, 5, 6, 7, 8, 9, 10, 11, 12, 13; Gloucester 7, 8; Hereford 6; Leeds 3; London (City) 6, 7, 9, 10; London (East End) 4, 6, 8, 10, 12; Manchester 13.

Kate Heron drew the town maps.

'Scenes of Rape' was drawn by Wally Conquy.

NOTE

Despite the urgency with which this book has been produced, it is inevitable that some of the situations described in it will have changed by the time it is published. Many threatened buildings will have fallen, while some we may hope will have been reprieved, and undoubtedly new threats will have arisen. Of course, also, many seriously threatened towns could not be covered in the selection. The authors do not intend that this book should be a substitute for further concern and action, either for them or for their readers, and they hope that readers will write with information about threats they know of and so join in the continuing battle.

Foreword

This is a devastating book. In my mind's ear I can hear the smooth tones of the committee man explaining why the roads must go where they do regardless of the humble old town they bisect. In my mind's eye I can see the swish perspective tricked up by the architect's firm to dazzle the local councillors. I see the tailored models walking past the plate glass, bent forward against a strong breeze. Round the corner I see senior citizens and youth representatives sipping Cinzano under a striped umbrella in the hot sunshine which always lends a Costa Brava look to architectural drawings. I hear words like 'complex', 'conurbation', 'precinct', 'pedestrianisation' and that other couple of words which mean total destruction, 'comprehensive development'. Places cease to have names, they become areas with a number. Houses become housing, human scale is abandoned.

We must put in something to please these tiresome people, the preservationists, and so we will leave, shorn of its surroundings, a Georgian building which has been praised in a guide book. If one of the pundits has said of a building 'not especially nice' then down it will come. And if he hasn't mentioned it there's no reason why we should preserve it.

What this book shows is the importance of the modest old buildings which act as foils to greater ones. It also shows little streets which had a life of their own and which were just taken for granted. And it shows, alas, too many faceless monsters in their place which bring increment to Mammon.

If there is some street or old shop in the market square, dock, factory or warehouse, barn or garden wall which you have passed often and taken for granted, do not expect to see it still there next week. Because it is not listed, because it is 'of no historic interest', the bulldozers will be in and part of your background will have gone for ever. As I look through this book I think that it is not only the developer who is to blame for the rape of Britain but also the 'yes-man' who wants to be on good terms with his committee, the architect who is his own public relations officer.

Finally, before it is too late, let us hold back the demolition men and follow the advice of the Department of the Environment—'Patch and mend. Make the best use of what is there already rather than destroy.'

The inevitable television question will be 'What good will this book do?' The answer is it opens our eyes to what is going on in the midst of us.

The quite unfaked and telling photographs, the authors' informed and forceful text, make a book which ought to grace every bookstall and be carried off in wire baskets from every supermarket which replaces an attractive building.

London, March 1975

John Betjeman

Top. *Ballance Street, Bath. Built in the 1770s, it was part of a network of small streets behind John Wood's grander Circus. All has been swept away by the City Council for new housing.*

Bottom. *The same view today.*

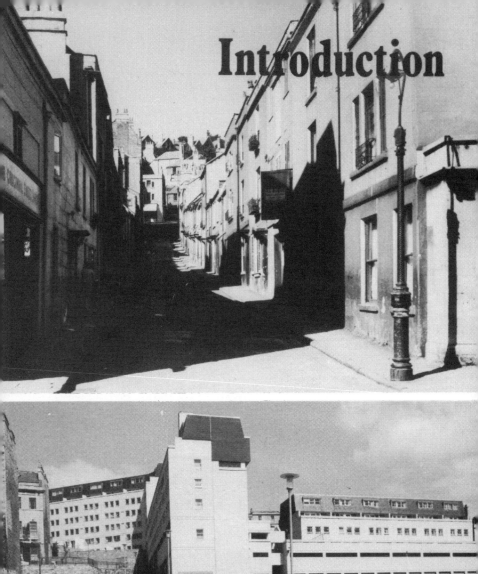

Introduction

Britain has not been invaded by an enemy power for more than nine hundred years. Her towns and cities suffered heavy damage from Nazi bombers during the Second World War but they had survived until then as a remarkably intact built history of the nation, so there was a lot to lose. Britain has not suffered from civil strife in the streets (except in Northern Ireland) and so it is fair to say that the damage to our towns since 1945 has been done by ourselves. The damage has been colossal and it has been carried out knowingly and effectively—almost as if there were an officially-sponsored competition to see how much of Britain's architectural heritage could be destroyed in thirty years. 1975 has been declared European Architectural Heritage Year to draw attention to and to protect our historic buildings: it takes a while for what has been obvious to the public for a long time to sink into the official mind. There has been a growing public awareness that our national architectural heritage is being eroded, and to the man in the street it has always looked as though the ravishing of our fine cities was being carried out largely for private profit but always with official blessing.

The curious feature of this vicious attack on the nation's cities is that it has all happened since 1945 and all since the passing of the Town and Country Planning Act of 1947, which was intended to assist in the creation of a better world. This book looks at just thirty examples of British towns that have suffered and are still in great danger. We draw attention to the historic buildings and areas that are likely to vanish in the next few years. With or without Heritage Year, Britain's architectural heritage is in grave danger. Our selection of towns ranges from the large cities of Northern England, like Manchester, where there are ten huge areas of comprehensive redevelopment that will totally eradicate much of the city's past, to small English towns where the loss of any more historic buildings would be a grievous blow. It would not have been difficult to include three hundred and thirty towns that have been in some way irreparably damaged by redevelopment since 1945.

What is most depressing about the state of our cities today is that they are all becoming monotonously alike. It is tragic that so much rebuilding has happened at a time when architecture and planning are at such a low ebb in Britain. In the majority of large town centre redevelopments money and mediocrity set the tone. At street level there is only the monotonous standardisation of the chain store shop fronts and, above, variations of the old mixture of concrete and glass. Sometimes the concrete is heavily marked by its timber boarding—this is known as texture: sometimes it is a mass of tiny pebbles—this is known as exposing the aggregate, what else? However it is finished, concrete is a joyless material, it is universal and it bears no more relationship to Aberdeen than to Addis Ababa. And it is now spread thickly all over Britain—long ribbons of it lead you into the multiple heaps of prefabricated units that now make up our town centres.

Britain's towns were once the visible expression of a way of life that had gradually evolved over the centuries. A walk down the main street of a small town in, say, East Anglia would show the changes in fortune, the civic pride, the progress of growth and gradual change. But change has accelerated and only up to the mid nineteenth century were the changes organic. The Industrial Revolution introduced the philosophy of laissez-faire, and the rampant philosophy of greed for material gain inevitably allied with a rapid rise in population. This, in turn, led to the rapid growth of towns and the despoliation of many historic cities in Europe. What was lost was that sense of a civic place that had reached its apotheosis in the eighteenth century. Areas of London, like Bloomsbury, managed to achieve the advantages of high-density living with the elegance of a planned layout that included open spaces and attractive streets. There was a realisation, up to the early twentieth century, that civilization had its roots in the city. The city was not simply somewhere to exploit for profit but a place where there could be a meeting of minds, a place where a random range of contacts could be made that held out the potential of a richness that had nothing to do with material gain.

The nineteenth century changed the form of many towns, but to our eyes now the work of the Victorians is infinitely more in keeping with the city than anything built in our own time. The destruction during the nineteenth century pales into insignificance alongside the licensed vandalism of the years 1950-75. Victorian 'improvers' were fumbling amateurs alongside today's professionally-aided merchants of greed. Accountancy and devotion to profit are the two spurs to redevelopment. Take some financiers and an architect who understands exactly how to squeeze the maximum amount of office space out of the smallest site and you have the basic elements of the recipe for a new town centre. It is the change in the scale that hits you about these new buildings. As soon as it was possible to span large areas with reinforced concrete the nature of building in towns changed. It was no longer possible to fit in alongside your neighbour because the modern style was such a complete break with the past. Arguments that suggest that a compromise modern style would do best in our towns miss the point. A compromise rarely produces anything of real distinction. The best modern building can find a place in Britain but it is rarely in the centre of an old town.

Our special concern in these pages is that the poor quality of most new buildings makes the repair and retention of Britain's older towns more essential. Our urban heritage is rich, but fragile, and once a building is demolished it can *never* be replaced. The full extent of Britain's archaeological and architectural heritage in her towns has only recently been recorded and listed. Since the 1947 Town and Country Planning Act, consolidated and strengthened by the 1968 and 1971 Acts, Investigators from the Department of the Environment have been making Lists of buildings of special historic or architectural interest that deserve statutory protection. All buildings dated before 1700 that survive in anything like their original condition are supposed to be Listed, as are most buildings built between 1700 and 1840. Buildings designed between 1840 and 1914 are not all Listed by any means. The Department says that those of outstanding quality and worth and the principal works of outstanding architects will be Listed. A start has been made on Listing the buildings between 1914 and 1939.

What does Listing mean? Buildings can be Listed for their exterior or interior features or for their associations with historic characters or events. Special types of buildings that have unique architectural or planning value are Listed

and buildings that are part of our social history like the industrial buildings, schools, hospitals, railway stations and town halls. Buildings are inspected and graded—Grade I, II* or II (in Scotland, Grade A or B), or put on a list of buildings that are considered of only local value. A Listed building (other than one on the local list) cannot be demolished or altered in any way that affects its character' without a 'Listed Building Consent' from the planning authority. The Secretary of State can call in for his own decision any application for consent to demolish. Owners of Listed buildings have a duty to preserve them: if they fail to look after them, a Repairs Notice can be served by the local authority, insisting on necessary repairs. If repairs are not carried out within two months, the authority can issue a Compulsory Purchase Order. If the building is being deliberately neglected because the owner wants to redevelop the site, it can be compulsorily purchased at a price that disregards its value for redevelopment.

Does all this legislation help? It certainly protects the major historic buildings, but in the recent example of the city of Bath, hundreds of good minor Georgian buildings were being bulldozed for the 'modernisation'—i.e. destruction—of the totality of the Georgian city. Are the right criteria being applied to the Listing of buildings? In 1947, the methodical listers could happily classify the major 'monuments' and they did not worry about where these buildings stood and who their neighbours were. Many good buildings were never Listed because of the uncertainty of the Listing criteria. Only during the 1960s, as awareness of the phenomenon known as the environment came into being, were the minor buildings—the settings for the great masterpieces—seen to be of value. The awareness of the value of whole streets and areas came about also because of the shattering speed of redevelopment in the 1960s and the traumatic effects on our towns of the new concrete disaster areas.

The Listing procedure is not yet adequate as it is seen as a very minor arm of the Government's environmental controls. The office responsible for Listing has a ludicrously small staff of twenty-one, and they are often running as hard as they can to keep up with the growing appreciation of old buildings and the staggering speed of their destruction. The Department of the Environment has said that it will take fifteen years to revise the Lists all over the country. By then, hundreds of valuable buildings could have been demolished. Certainly, as yet unlisted Victorian and Edwardian buildings are particularly vulnerable. Local authorities are often reluctant or unable for financial reasons to purchase compulsorily a neglected or dangerous historic structure. Unless Parliamentary time is found to strengthen the law in this respect, the Listing procedure will lack the support it needs. Also, if more buildings are to be saved, there must be more DOE staff to speed up the Listing procedure. For major cities the resurveys can take up to two years and tie up the limited number of investigators at the expense of other places.

There is no full list of historic towns that could give an accurate picture of what is happening in all of them. The Council for British Archaeology produced its own list in 1965 which contained 324 towns, of which 51 were considered to be of special importance. The Council's initial list included 660 places that were of some historical value. The shorter list and in particular the 50 special towns were thought to be good enough to be of 'national importance' and to be specially in need of careful treatment in any planning or redevelopment proposals. One-third of the towns in this book were on that special list and the photographs that follow show how much special care has been taken in their redevelopment. The Council's list probably appeared too late: by the mid-sixties the property boom was well underway and even local authorities were caught up in the euphoria of profit-making. Mere concern for history had little support.

Another aspect of the planning legislation conceived to improve the urban environment that somehow went badly wrong was the use of the Comprehensive Development Area procedure. The three letters CDA will often crop up in this book; they symbolise all the unpleasantly destructive aspects of town planning. The procedure was designed to enable planning authorities to go beyond mere planning control and by Compulsory Purchase Order acquire any properties that they might see fit to buy and demolish to secure the rebuilding of outworn areas. Usually the areas selected for this kind of approach are old city centres that are to be replaced by the concrete vision of the planning officer brought up on Abercrombie and the Ville Radieuse. Behind the thinking that accepts the CDA procedure is the mind that seriously believes that the centre of Manchester should look like a futuristic vision or a barbaric new city borrowed from Le Corbusier.

Money and traffic are the two other pressures that have changed the towns. It has become possible for a small gang of developers to look at our cities as units of commercial space. Compromise is not a word that exists in a cost accountant's vocabulary; planners are expected to—and do—help find sites for the exact amount of square footage necessary for retailers and office managers to squeeze the maximum profit out of their new locations. Since 1970, when a Conservative Government returned to power, nearly 30 million square feet of offices were given development permits in London alone. (During the Second World War 9.5 million square feet of offices were destroyed.) With the rise in office rents between 1970 and 1973 the net capital value of office space generated by the issue of Office Development Permits is estimated at not less than £860 million. With whole areas like Dockland, Covent Garden, Southwark's riverside and Soho ripe for development, London stands to add yet more to the private fortunes of a few property companies. Despite changes in Government and increases in taxation, there is a well-established breed of men in the City of London who believe that property is still the best form of long-term investment. This inevitably means that property continues to attract funds from the pension and insurance market which makes it a dangerous field for unwary politicians to tamper with. The physical manifestations of these financial machinations are simply seen in investment terms. What the new buildings look like and where they are sited is almost immaterial. As always it must be the client that calls the tune and Britain's new breed of patrons have eyes only for their bank statements. The result is a giant-scale visual disaster which is being gallantly challenged by protesters working as best they can in their spare time.

Traffic is the other main reason for the restructuring of so many towns. Despite

12

Scenes of Rape

the inflationary cost of motoring, roads are still being built to meet the target figure of 35 million cars in thirty years' time. Behind this has been the belief that you don't restrain the car. Even as the possible twilight of the motor age approaches, the certainty that cars must be allowed in the cities is the prevalent planning doctrine. If they can't be squeezed into the city, the city itself must be radically altered to make room. Parallel to this axiom, that the car must be allowed to move freely in the city, is the naive belief in the virtues of pedestrianisation. To pedestrianise a few streets it has sometimes been necessary to build new roads that destroy large parts of the town. Pedestrianisation should go hand-in-hand with traffic management, both trying to find ad hoc temporary solutions to make life more comfortable, without indulging in permanently damaging closed streets or new roads. At amazing cost, a road is being built in Glasgow that will save ten minutes on a journey from the city to the airport: ten minutes saved and an enormous swathe of the city destroyed forever. A walk or, even more unnerving, a drive through the centre of Birmingham should be enough to demonstrate that architectural aberrations are no longer confined to dreams. The streets are full of massive, endless, faceless new buildings. A desert has been created where once there was a city.

Already in Britain there are people who have no memory of their birthplace, no links left with the generations before them and no visual impressions of anything beyond their concrete balconies and the concrete balconies of their neighbours. The visual poverty of our new surroundings throws into relief the need for retention of the buildings of the past. As Lord Clark has said, 'No society can cut off its deep roots and destroy its history without forever impoverishing its spirit.'

In the pages that follow the 'rape' of our towns can be seen taking a variety of forms, from the most obvious and brutal obliterations of nearly all that was there before in Manchester or Huddersfield; to

the destruction of the integrity of the town by intrusive and unsympathetic development in Edinburgh or Bath; or the destruction of outstanding individual buildings and pieces of historic townscape in Frome or Berwick; or the more subtly insidious emasculation of the character of historic buildings in Salisbury. London receives special treatment: the City represents commercial pressures at their most extreme, acting on the most historic urban area in the country; Soho offers a detailed case study of the growth and threatened disintegration of the heart of a living city; and the East End appears as an illustration of wasted opportunity in the treatment of a historic area that has been subject to progressive destruction over a long period of time.

In the case of one town, Ashford, the attitude of those who are rebuilding the town is allowed to speak for itself in the words and pictures of an advertising supplement proclaiming the birth of Ashford as a town of the future.

A final section, 'And...', picks out at random individual threats to fine buildings all over Britain, to show that the process we are describing is happening everywhere. It would have been easy to have produced double the number and readers will be able to think of their own examples.

'Rape' will doubtless sometimes be felt too strong a term and we may be thought to have understated the problems of conserving and paying for our historic towns. Nor does this book present a picture of the good things that are happening in many places. We have deliberately shown the darker side of the coin. But if we have chosen to reveal the worst, the facts ought not to have made our task so easy. And the facts speak for themselves. Whatever the extenuating circumstances, whoever or whatever is responsible, many of our most important historic towns are being or have been ravished. We have no doubt that the protest which the revelation of these facts represents will strike a responsive chord in all those who care deeply about what is happening to our heritage.

Aberdeen

Aberdeen has always been known as the granite flower of the north, a place of sobriety, learning and culture reflected in the modest grandeur of long, wide, classical Union Street and in the smart, severe grey granite which is the uniform building material throughout the city. In places sudden falls in the level of the land give rise to unexpected vistas or the intricately-woven winding tunnel streets characteristic of dense urban surroundings at their most exciting.

In the last two years Aberdeen has become the Offshore Capital of Europe, servicing and supplying the oil rigs of the North Sea oil bonanza. More than 200 companies in and around Aberdeen are directly involved in the offshore oil industry. The tower cranes are beginning to rise in the hinterland of small streets behind Union Street, starkly heralding the imminent arrival of the dominating, alien office blocks that will be their lasting successors. House prices in Aberdeen are among the highest in the country, reflecting the intense but short-lived pressures that

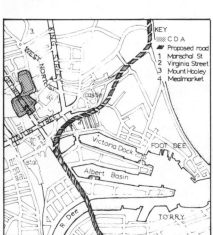

KEY
CDA
Proposed road
1 Marischal St
2 Virginia Street
3 Mount Hooley
4 Mealmarket

THE WEDDING BELL

will almost certainly leave a wrecked Aberdeen in their wake.

In George Street, the city's second main thoroughfare, the bulbous bulk of the Co-op's Norco House, looking like a many-layered caterpillar, stands in almost surreal discord with its ordinary street surroundings. It is the most conspicuous advertisement of the CDA in the heart of the city, where extensive clearance is already going on. Nearby numbers of important buildings stand

empty. In the office of the Director of Town Planning a chart on the wall shows how Aberdeen's office space is to grow by 56 per cent in the next few years. At least 1½ million square feet of offices will be built by 1978. A foretaste of what is to come is offered by the ugly, aggresively horizontal concrete developer's office block at the corner of West North Street and Mealmarket Street just built for Teeslands Investments, a subsidiary of the Charterhouse Group. The rest of Aberdeen waits apprehensively, wondering where the office developers will strike next.

A short time ago the old fishing village of Old Torry in the southern suburbs of the city was to be designated a Conservation Area. The intention was to restore the old houses, plant trees and make Old Torry an attractive seaside village for people to live in. The old houses, many of them two-storey tenements with large drying lofts once used

1.   *Virginia Street. This remarkable and rare eighteenth-century house, Listed Grade A, will be demolished with other granite houses for the oil men's new dual carriageway.*
2.   *Footdee, once a fishing village, is a Conservation Area. Will it survive as oil development surrounds it on all sides?*
3.   *Strong granite houses in Gallowgate likely to be replaced by offices for the oil companies.*
4.   *Listed houses in Upper Kirkgate, to be destroyed in the City's CDA.*
5.   *New-style George Street. The protuberant design of the new Co-op.*
6.   *Torry, an ancient fishing village older than Aberdeen itself. It was on the brink of becoming a Conservation Area when it was totally destroyed for Shell UK's refinery.*
7.   *Solidity and grandeur in Aberdeen's characteristic granite, going for the new road.*
8.   *Early nineteenth century houses with arcaded ground floors in King Street. Disciplined urban space to be broken apart by the new road.*
9.   *Warehouse in Virginia Street, to be demolished for the new road.*
10.   *Telford's bridge carrying Marischal Street over Virginia Street, to be demolished for 'Oil Way'.*

18

10

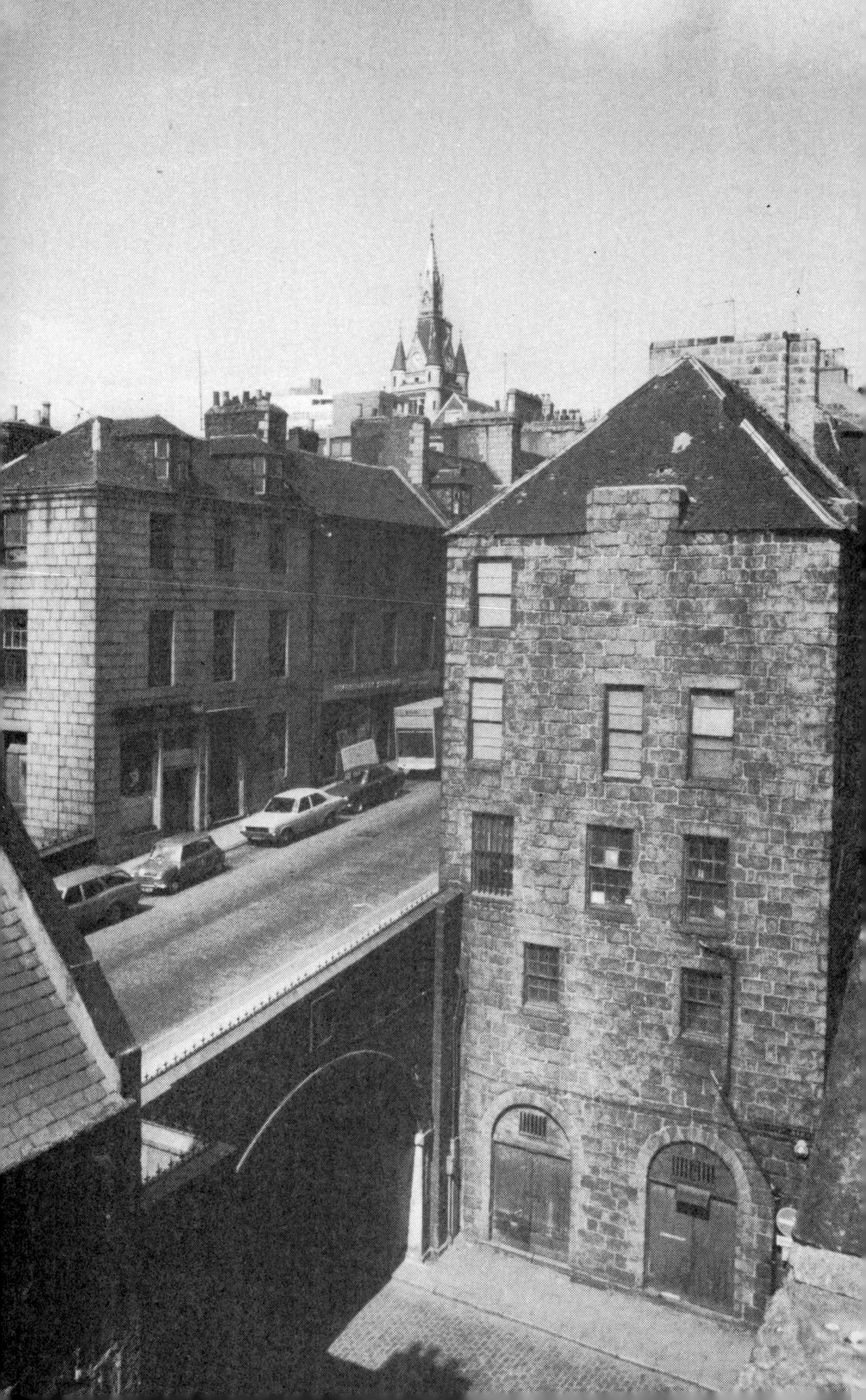

12

for fish and nets, would have converted well into small flats of considerable character. In the spring of 1974 the whole village was demolished to make way for a new Shell oil refinery. How soon will the similar Conservation Area fishing village of Footdee next to the docks go the same way?

To link the Torry oil works in the south to a similar plant in the north the City is building a road through the centre of Aberdeen. The road will plough through Castlehill and demolish the northern side of Virginia Street, which has tall granite houses including an important early eighteenth century house Listed Grade A. It will also take in its wake Telford's stone bridge which carries Marischal Street down the hill over Virginia Street. The whole size of this road and its related works seems to be well beyond both the present and future needs of Aberdeen: at Mount Hooley a

site has been cleared that will become a traffic roundabout as large as Hyde Park Corner. South from Mount Hooley a dual carriageway runs down demolished West North Street and will soon break across formal King Street and down Commercial Street to join the new road from Torry.

11. *Mount Hooley, the site of a major new roundabout bigger than Hyde Park Corner.*
12. *Victorian church in a leafy park below Union Street, derelict and likely to be demolished.*
13. *Small vernacular granite houses like these in Nelson Street have been cleared in their hundreds to make way for new roads.*

Bath

Bath, one of the finest and most famous cities in Europe, has been the classic case of the urban destroyer's handiwork. The obvious landmarks like the Circus and the Royal Crescent remain immune. But the whole setting of the Georgian city has been ransacked. Whole areas of perfect small- and medium-sized Georgian stone terraces, equivalent to the architectural heritage of several towns, have entirely vanished in the last decade and in their place are rising crass monstrosities in violent discord with the character of what remains. Following a national outcry in 1973, the headlong progress of comprehensive redevelopment has been restrained. The Conservation Area has been enlarged and 700 buildings are to be added to the List. The Government and the Bath Preservation Trust are now directly involved with the city authorities in deciding the city's future.

The outcry proclaimed the lessons that the case of Bath holds for every historic city: competition for regional shopping and office development is incompatible with the survival of a historic city; the

1. *Ballance Street. The kind of future being forged for the city in 1973.*
2. *Morford Street, still derelict.*
3. *The setting of Pulteney Bridge, marred by the Beaufort Hotel.*

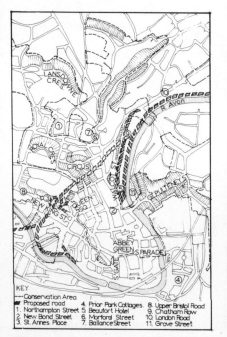

KEY
--- Conservation Area
▬ Proposed road
1. Northampton Street
2. New Bond Street
3. St. Annes Place
4. Prior Park Cottages
5. Beaufort Hotel
6. Morford Street
7. Ballance Street
8. Upper Bristol Road
9. Chatham Row
10. London Road
11. Grove Street

destruction of towns for supposed public benefits is not what the public wants; local authorities cannot be left to decide the fate of towns that are part of a national heritage. But we have yet to see that the lessons of Bath are being effectively applied in Bath itself.

Right in the centre, where a vast area has already been cleared for the huge square box of the Beaufort Hotel and the monstrously modernistic new law courts, stands New Bond Street. It is all that is holding the two halves of riverside Bath together. To the east of it is a new shopping development, to the west the Beaufort Hotel. It has now been decided that this gently curving early nineteenth century street will have to go. Still under direct threat and decaying even more rapidly is St Ann's Place of *c*.1770, planned to go for road access to New King Street despite being in the Conservation Area. In a similar condition are Prior Park Cottages—part of Ralph Allen's Lower Town of *c*.1740, very likely by John Wood I. The cottages were Listed in January 1973 but Avon County wants them demolished for road widening. Also at risk within the Conservation Area are Nos. 4, 5 and 6 Northampton Street, by John Pinch, *c*.1793-1800. Finally, the major threat of the Relief Road/Tunnel still remains, resulting in continuing blight along the route—as in 'the Walcot Street area, where the last Georgian terraces with gardens running down to the river survive.

4. *The unique Real Tennis Court of 1770, still derelict.*
5. *The early nineteenth century New Bond Street, the strand that holds two sides of Bath together, soon to be snapped.*
6. *Venetian window in a house in the Upper Bristol Road, probably to be demolished.*
7. *St Anne's Place, an intimate late eighteenth century court in the line of a proposed road.*
8. *Prior Park Cottages, built in 1740 for Ralph Allen's masons, to be demolished for road works.*
9. *Bedford Street, off London Road. Early nineteenth century cottages still under threat.*
10. *Northampton Street. The right side is to go for a new school.*
11. *Chatham Row, a fine group of 1760 houses, blighted by road plans.*

Berwick

As a fortified city Berwick is unique. It has retained intact its Elizabethan ramparts and it still has the air of an eighteenth-century garrison town inside the walls. It has a remarkable architectural heritage—one in ten of its buildings is Listed. Fought over by the English and Scots for over four hundred years, Berwick was last officially sacked in 1389. Threats to the town today could destroy far more than any Border skirmishes.

The town is still suffering from the foolish planning decision of 1928 which kept the Great North Road inside the walls when the new Tweed bridge was built. Today the traffic thunders under the seventeenth century Scot's Gate and through the town. Any attempt to deal

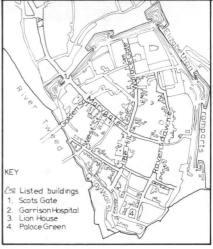

KEY

⌂ Listed buildings
1. Scots Gate
2. Garrison Hospital
3. Lion House
4. Palace Green

with the congestion that results from this by widening roads can only mean the destruction of Listed buildings.

The first candidate for improvement is the approach road to the bridge. The DOE wants to demolish one side of Golden Square—which contains an 1820 Grammar School—and the gabled seventeenth century house on the corner. Any road widening within the walls will inevitably turn the Scot's Gate into a bottleneck, making its destruction only a matter of time. Facing each other across Marygate are two hotels, the Salmon Hotel, 1912, a jolly piece of Edwardiana, and the Old Waterloo Hotel. Both of these could go for a supermarket and behind the Salmon are the remains of the oldest inn in Berwick, the Feathers, 1668, which would also be destroyed. One large supermarket sits at the bottom of Marygate in a sea of devastation, a grotesque brick box housing the Co-op, accepted by the Council after the Co-op threatened to go elsewhere if its design was refused. A neighbouring row of eighteenth-century houses in Westgate continues to decay.

The dereliction that is threatening to destroy Westgate is endangering many other parts of the town. A Grade I eighteenth-century building on the Quay Walls, a vital part of the townscape and derelict for years, is being restored by the Berwick Preservation Trust with Government help. But the equally important Lion House overlooking the Elizabethan ramparts is to be allowed to fall down, and eighteenth-century cottages on Palace Green and the Garrison Hospital of 1720 seem certain to go the same way.

1.   *The fine character of Marygate, gradually being eroded by anonymous commercial architecture.*
2.   *The seventeenth-century Scot's Gate links two Elizabethan bastions. The Great North Road runs beneath the arch towards the spire of the eighteenth-century Town Hall.*
3.   *103-107 Marygate, wanted by the DOE for a road widening scheme.*
4.   *The Co-op building. A dreadful intrusion in a walled town where every space used to have a meaning.*
5.   *Palace Green. Cottages the Council is considering demolishing for housing.*
6.   *Rum Puncheon café, Marygate, also to be demolished for the road.*
7.   *Eighteenth-century houses in Westgate Street, about to be engulfed.*
8.   *The early eighteenth century Garrison Hospital in Ravensdown stands rotting behind its high garden wall.*
9.   *Lion House, one of the best and most strikingly sited houses in Berwick and Listed Grade II*.*

Beverley

Apart from the obvious glory of Beverley's Minster, the attractions of the town are small-scale and modest. Brick and pantile houses reveal the history of the town's fortunes in the variety and richness of their craftsmanship. The town today still reflects the quiet and steady growth of a place that has been for years an undisturbed centre of a prosperous region. Georgian and older houses in generous gardens, and the still intact medieval street pattern, underlie the town's richness. By the end of the eighteenth century Hull had become the major centre for trade and industry in the region and the subsequent growth of Beverley was limited to some small housing estate developments from the end of the nineteenth century.

Today the spine of related buildings and spaces that runs from St Mary's via Ladygate, Toll Gavel, Wednesday Market and Eastgate to the Minster is severely endangered by traffic. Increased mobility has allowed Beverley a new regional significance which has put heavy pressure on the old fabric of this remarkable town. In 1968 the road 'improvements' began and the then local authority destroyed the enclosure of the northern end of the market place to create the new Sow Hill road; now the intimacy of the market leaks out into a desolate distant prospect of the bus station and the new road junction. A further road is planned to cut through the area on the northern side of Walkergate. This bears no relation to the traffic pressures that will be generated by the imminent opening of the Humber Bridge, which will send a vastly increased amount of traffic rushing through the town. When the Council does get round to dealing with this assault, it will be with a bypass to the south-west of the town. The pointlessness of the Walkergate road is now all but admitted, but the new planning authority says it is going ahead with it

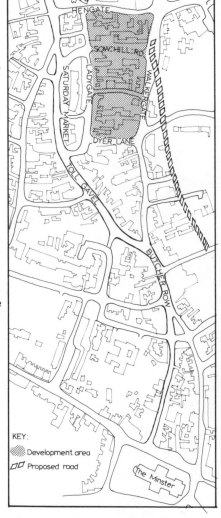

KEY:
Development area
Proposed road

1, 2. The old intimacy of the market place has been destroyed by the new road leading to the desolate bus station.
3, 4. Ladygate, leading out of the corner of the market, may be developed as a parking and shopping area. Blight has followed in the wake of the plans, 3.
5. Acres of tarmac have already ruined the setting of St Mary's Church.
6. This fine Georgian house now overlooks parked cars and may go for roads.

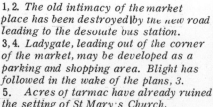

because the plans have gone too far to be dropped.

The supermarket syndrome is also raising its head in Beverley. For several years the Council has been buying up small sites to create a comprehensive five-acre holding of old lanes and houses bounded by Ladygate, Walkergate, Hengate and Dyer Lane. Originally there were proposals for a new parking and shopping area that would 'inject new life' into the shopping facilities in the centre of Beverley. Since then the Council has been having second thoughts, but still indecision over the proposals has produced a large area of blight in the centre of the town. The future of the area will only be resolved with the result of

the public inquiry into the road proposals in the spring of 1975. Large-scale redevelopment of any sort would be highly destructive of Beverley's quality and character. The whole nature of the tight street pattern and the historical continuity of the central area must remain sacred. The subtle rules that have to date directed the evolution of the town still apply. Beverley is too good to be damaged for the transient benefits of supermarkets and traffic.

7.   *Road widening threatens Ladygate.*
8, 9.   *The salvaged remains of the fifteenth-century Dominican Friary, only now to be restored.*

Brighton

Ever since the Prince Regent made the Pavilion into his own Oriental fun palace, Brighton has been on the map as a centre of seaside amusement. While it may lack the scholarly architectural consistency of somewhere like Bath, it has an incredible variety of Regency and Victorian architecture that gives a very definite and coherent character to the town. Because it has still an immense potential for pleasure and profit it has received its share of the developers' attention.

The biggest development to hit Brighton is, of course, the Marina—an exclusive paradise for the expensive sailing classes. There is no question that the large-scale flats and service buildings will ruin forever the peaceful Undercliffe Walk from Kemp Town along the white chalk cliffs to Rottingdean. Less certain is the effect of a series of service roads that will bring masses of Marina traffic through the sensitive areas of the town. While the cost of the Marina spirals towards the £100 million mark, Brighton Corporation is reluctant to save the West Pier at a cost of perhaps one million pounds.

It is from the piers that there is a good view of the sea front, no longer that remarkable series of terraces with the Downs as a backcloth. The town is now dominated by high blocks of commercial ugliness. Churchill Square and its neighbouring slab blocks have a crushing effect on the neighbouring streets; tiny Regency houses find themselves looking into the dark cavernous openings of multi-storey car parks. The proposed conference centre that will complete

1.   *West Pier. For sale at £1: no bids.*
2.   *The Marina. Despite soaring building costs and furious controversy this massive development continues.*
3.   *Coast Guard cottages, to be demolished for the Marina approach roads.*
4.   *St James's Street, once the lively high street of Kemp Town.*
5.   *The same view today.*
6.   *St Bartholomew's Church. Diminutive neighbours that enhance its scale are slowly disappearing.*
7.   *Brighton Station, with its fine curved train sheds. BR plans redevelopment.*

Churchill Square and be a neighbour to the Grand Hotel has the difficult task of fitting space for 5,000 delegates into the town without further wrecking the character that visitors come to see.

Arriving in Brighton is unlikely to be a very pleasant experience if the proposals for the redevelopment of the Victorian railway station with its fine curving iron and glass roof are allowed by the new Council to proceed any further. British Rail's ambitions for a huge office complex seem unlikely to be realised in the present economic climate, but the plan for a hypermarket on part of the site could bring a completely unnecessary increase in traffic. Surely a hypermarket belongs, if anywhere, to the outer suburbs. The area to the east of the station, between the station, the Steine and the London Road, is being bought into, though the Council has turned down a scheme in Kensington Gardens. It is a small-scale area of narrow streets, small houses and markets where you can buy anything from secondhand crystal sets to army surplus camouflage jackets. Parts of the area, like Kensington Gardens, are full of these fringe shops that must have flourished in the Lanes before the Lanes became chic. Any chance of these off-beat uses disappearing and the tiny but attractive cottages being demolished must be resisted. The mixture of seediness and splendour is part of Brighton, along with the fish and chips, Brighton rock, the antique shops and the casinos. The Church Street-Jubilee Street area near the Royal Pavilion, which the Brighton Society has described as 'exquisite Victoriana', is endangered by the large rebuilding scheme that could bring modern commercial architecture to the doorstep of the Pavilion, sweeping away the gradual accretions of the last century. Kemp Town survives in a very patchy way. The grander buildings on the sea front are sufficiently good to appeal even to the councillors; the less obvious qualities of the minor supporting streets are not appreciated by Brighton. Several pointless demolitions have taken place in and around St James's Street.

Looking down on Brighton from the high railway viaduct there is always the exciting moment when the great brick ark of St Bartholomew's Church comes into view. Even the extraordinary scale of this astonishing building rising out of the tiny streets is endangered. The

demolition of houses in Ann Street has already given the church the look of an abandoned giant.

8. *North Street, an area of small shops and markets that will be lost if planned major developments go ahead.*
9. *Church Street–Jubilee Street area, invaded by redevelopment.*
10. *1795 Gothic almshouses, empty and derelict for years.*

1

Bristol

A walk round Bristol is a chastening experience, for there can be few cities in which so many historic and beautiful buildings are being destroyed; few cities in which literally hundreds of eighteenth- and nineteenth-century buildings stand desolate and broken, waiting only for the so far readily granted permission before they are demolished.

Lodge Street presents a sight which can be repeated over and over again: indeed, whichever way you choose to walk it is impossible not to find it repeated. The buildings in Lodge Street are Listed but it is hard to believe that they have any future; a few more months and the Council will put them out of their misery with a Dangerous Structure Notice. Lodge Street is on its own but one Conservation Area, the Portland Square area, consists almost entirely of houses of the same type, threatened in large numbers. The south side of Brunswick Square, built in 1766, has a curious planning history. Finally reprieved at the last moment by the Secretary of State, acting against the advice of his own inspector, the buildings are theoretically saved for posterity. The

photograph was taken almost a year after the decision. Having escaped the speedy despatch of the demolition men, the buildings are being left to die by themselves. Pritchard Street, St Paul's Street, Gloucester Street and Newfoundland Street are all in a similar condition. The area was originally developed for residential use, its proximity to the city centre gradually turning it over to light industrial uses and multiple occupancy; further damaged in the war, it now faces the sterner onslaught of the commercial developer's interests; the picture of Brunswick Square shows the tide almost upon it. Being made a Conservation Area will only help in part as the increasing trend in Bristol is to permit demolition of this type of building as long as the facade is retained, or even rebuilt in facsimile, a sop to the conservationist conscience.

Right in the centre of the Clifton Conservation Area stands Boyce's Buildings. One of the earliest of the Clifton terraces, it was built in 1763. Originally a balanced composition with central pediment, the right-hand wing was destroyed

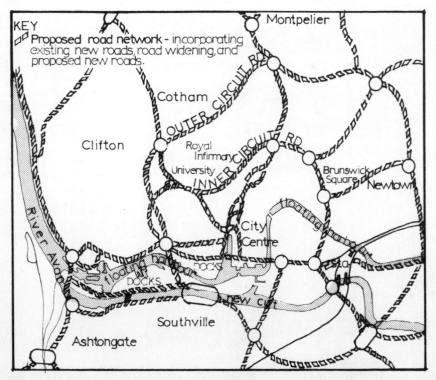

by bombing. The rest, with its fine Gibbs surrounds to the windows, typical of the earlier Bristol buildings, has survived two public inquiries to little profit; and yet if the shops in front were removed they would need very little to restore them to their original appearance.

A different story can be told of Nos. 66, 68 and 70 Prince Street, built in 1725, probably to the designs of William Halfpenny and John Strahan. These are perhaps architecturally the finest buildings threatened with demolition in the city. They stand in the way of the notorious Inner Circuit Road which ironically enough is intended to bypass Queen Square so that it can be closed to traffic again, having been split by the present road before the war. It is intended to run through the gap between the two warehouses and then bridge St Augustine's Road, which is immediately behind the houses, and on away towards the Hotwell Road.

The Outer Circuit Road, planned since 1966, has now become a self-perpetuating fact and its seems that nothing can stop its progress. It will swathe through old streets, houses and the docks in a great ring round the city on the classic pattern.

1.   *The magnificent Baroque facade of a house in Prince Street.*
2.   *Listed Lodge Street, decayed to the point where a Dangerous Structures Notice could be served.*
3.   *Brunswick Square has been officially 'saved'. The picture tells another story.*
4.   *This superb rock-faced warehouse opposite the threatened buildings in Prince Street is the subject of a demolition application.*
5.   *Georgian streets adjacent to Brunswick Square, also rotting away.*
6.   *Detail of facade in Prince Street.*
7.   *Boyce's Buildings in Clifton has survived bomb damage and two public inquiries. It seems it will not survive the new Bristol fashion of calculated neglect.*
8.   *There is nothing else left in the city like these 1725 houses in Prince Street. A road is planned to go through them.*

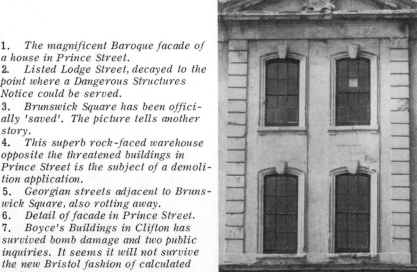

The road problem generally is a serious one in Bristol, for the town map makes provision for widening every major radial. The A38 in Stokes Croft is already largely a scene of dereliction, while the Whiteladies Road, a pleasant, tree-lined shopping street containing a very fine variety of early Victorian buildings, is marked down for major widening, which will entirely destroy its present character.

In 1964, Bristol gained its first tower block, the Robinson Building beside Bristol Bridge. This was an event of major importance for the city. Previously the vertical emphasis had been given by the towers and spires of the many city churches. A view today tells a different story. The trick now is to pick out any churches at all. Bristol is a boom town, the regional centre for government and national organisations alike. This puts an intolerable pressure on the central area for more office space. It is said that Bristol already has more multi-storey car parks than any other city; it now appears to be going for the office block record as well.

Churches and chapels stand out among the fine buildings awaiting the attentions of the pick-axe. Lewins Mead Chapel of 1788 stands in the way of an office development. The Portland Chapel of 1792 appears to be beyond redemption and indeed the Methodist Church, which still owns it, obtained consent for its demolition three years ago. Holy Trinity Church, designed by Thomas Rickman in 1829, is also threatened, like Butterfield's High Victorian Chapel, and the Congregational Chapel in Avonmouth has just been demolished.

9. The eighteenth-century Lewins Mead Chapel is being edged out.
10. Today's city centre viewed from Brandon Hill. Not long ago the view of Bristol was famous for its spires.
11. The road that would cut across Prince Street is just a part of the massive proposed new road system. It would eventually link up with this swirl of road in front of the docks.

Property developers and big companies are not the only villains in Bristol. Public institutions like the University and the Bristol Royal Infirmary also play their part. Ensconced in huge areas on either side of St Michael's Hill, and secure in the assumption that anything they do must be for the good of the community, they have slowly swallowed all that is old and small around them. At the top of the hill on the right-hand side is a long range of eighteenth- and nineteenth-century buildings still in reasonable condition. It is reported that the hospital authorities have recently stripped the lead off the roofs of the remaining inhabited ones to prevent it from being stolen. The site is intended for nurses' accommodation. Why not use the houses?

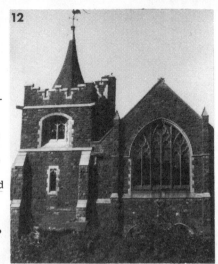

Bristol's docks were the principal gateway to the New World until the early part of the nineteenth century, when a huge new area of docks was created by diverting the Avon—a response to the rise of competition from Liverpool. A great variety of nineteenth century brick warehouses still stand in exciting proximity to the city centre. The docks are to be closed to all commercial traffic by 1980 and are destined to disappear under a bewildering jungle of roads and flyovers, one of the chief victims of the Outer Circuit Road plan.

On the city's outskirts stands the marvellous medieval-Jacobean-Georgian mansion Ashton Court. Bought very cheaply after the war by the Council on the understanding that it would be preserved, it has been seriously neglected and now stands in a deplorable condition. The Council has at last voted £450,000 towards restoration, but no use has yet been decided for the house. Its future is still far from secure.

12. *The Congregational Chapel, Avonmouth, now demolished.*
13. *Christmas Steps. This curiously medieval remnant will be shattered when the Council demolishes the house on the left.*
14. *St Michael's Hill is under assault from University and Hospital Board.*
15. *The Portland Chapel, abandoned.*
16. *Inside, a fragment of its eighteenth-century elegance survives as the gallery floats over a sea of smashed monuments and broken pews.*
17. *A fine seventeenth-century house stands stranded and neglected amid new University developments.*
18. *Turner Edward's Bond No. 1 is typical of Bristol's fine nineteenth-century warehouses, now becoming obsolete.*
19. *Ashton Court dates from the fifteenth to the nineteenth centuries. After years of neglect in Council ownership restoration plans are afoot, but its future use is yet to be decided.*

Cardiff

The late eighteenth century and early nineteenth century industrialisation of the valleys north of Cardiff set off a boom that turned a small market town dominated by its Castle into the capital of Wales and the largest coal-exporting port in the world. The growth of the city owed a good deal to the local magnate, the second Marquess of Bute, who created first Butetown, then Bute Street and Mount Stuart Square, as southward extensions of the old town, and built the docks. The 1870s saw the building of large Victorian commercial palaces in a mixture of styles on the medieval street pattern. The finest aspect of the development of this period is a splendid series of covered shopping arcades. The Castle still dominates the older area of Cardiff, its enlargement and restoration a spectacular example of the decorative work of the Victorian architect William Burges. To the east of the castle in Cathays Park is the unique Baroque Portland stone Civic Centre, begun in 1904, finally giving expression to Cardiff's status as an important city.

The decline of coal has created areas of decay and dereliction in the city. Some of the Bute Docks have been filled in and there are several important dock buildings in danger. Because of the uncertain future of this mostly disused port, the Bute warehouse of 1861 with its iron colonnaded ground floor, a massive gabled warehouse at right angles to it and the flamboyant French Gothic Dock Office of 1896 (architect William Frame, Burges's local assistant), a landmark on the Pier head site—are all at risk.

To give Cardiff a 1970s image, the Corporation has made a deal with developers Ravenseft. The City made 230 acres of city centre a redevelopment area and an enormous area of the whole city is to become a new commercial centre. Even the developers think the scale of the redevelopment somewhat ambitious and, finding it difficult to raise the cash, want to pull out. The CDA proposals emphasise the importance of retaining the Victorian facades and the scale of the Queen Street-Hayes Street-St Mary Street area with their intercommunicating arcades. The arcades are rightly seen as a major feature of the existing shopping centre and their principle is to be extended in the new development. Yet despite a certain recognition of the old town's Victorian commercial character, the south end

of St Mary Street between the important curved Gothic front of the Great Western Hotel (c. 1875-79) and Wood Street is liable to disappear. The elaborate twin-domed building next to the Gothic Cardiff Building Society is definitely to be demolished and this must put in question the rest of the block, including the lively Venetian Gothic of the Prince of Wales Theatre (c. 1878), facing Wood Street. At the bottom of Woodgate, to the rear of the grand Royal Hotel, with its rustication and French mansard roof, is a vacant site being used as a car park. A large signboard proclaims the future erection of a tower block which will effectively overshadow the Royal Hotel and, more importantly, the GPO building behind. This is an elaborate classical Portland stone building with a Flemish Renaissance gabled and turreted skyline, by Henry Tanner, 1896. The fact that the tower block would be off St Mary Street's axis is hardly an excuse for its soaring height: so much for retaining the scale of the existing environment. This sort of insensitive development already rears up on the Friary site, disastrously competing with the Cathays Park landmark of the City Hall clock tower. On Queen Street, the imposing front of the Park Hotel (1885, by Habershone and Fawckner) could well go the same way: a slab block has been proposed for the site. The great sweep of parkland along the river is one of Cardiff's greatest assets, retaining a feeling of open country in the city centre.

Part of the new road scheme now threatens to break up the traditional relationship of town and Castle. Castle Street is

to be widened into a six-lane urban highway cutting off a large chunk of lawn in front of the Castle and also involving the realignment of the boundary wall with its remarkable animal figures. A similar brutal cross-road has already severed the sequence of Windsor Place and St Andrew's Crescent. Also possibly threatened by roads or redevelopment is the stucco-faced old Custom House of 1845 on the corner of Custom House Street.

Cardiff could be completely changed by the massive nature of its redevelopment, and the question must be asked: Is it necessary? Even the developers are uncertain of its profitability. Perhaps this means it was never necessary in the first place.

1. *Uncertainty hangs over the future of this gabled warehouse seen from the iron colonnade of the Bute Warehouse.*
2. *The flamboyant silhouette of the Dock Office on the pier head, threatened along with other fine dock buildings.*
3. *The Prince of Wales Theatre.*
4. *The stucco Custom House of 1845.*
5. *Henry Tanner's GPO building with its gables and turrets will be overshadowed by a new tower block.*
6. *Onion domes and lively facades in St Mary Street, earmarked for destruction.*
7. *The Park Hotel, 1885, to be replaced by a slab block.*

Cheltenham

2

3

4

5

Cheltenham was a Regency spa that grew well into the Victorian period. A Royal visit lasting for five weeks in 1788 gave the expanding town the seal of fashionable approval. It prospered as a summer resort in an atmosphere of leafy elegance. The Lansdown and Montpellier estates developed as the first English garden city with the houses set amongst the formal avenues and gardens. On the Pittville estate the speculator Joseph Pitt achieved in the broad lines of tree-lined streets a perfect setting for the Greek Revival architecture embellished with elaborate ironwork. Cheltenham continued to grow well into the 1840s with large villas at Bayshill, which became, as the popularity of the spa declined, perfect residences for retired Indian Army officers and Colonial administrators.

The spacious elegance of Cheltenham is under threat of gradual erosion. Large villas are empty and derelict and the stucco fronts of the houses and terraces are crumbling and in need of constant maintenance. New developments are too often unresponsive to the nature of the town. A monolithic shopping development in the High Street already dwarfs its neighbours and introduces an ugly horizontal emphasis into a street of individual late-Georgian buildings. Several of the Regency villas near the centre have been converted into offices or hotels, while those in outlying suburbs are being turned into flats. Ugly rear extensions and asphalt over the gardens are the unfortunate results of a policy that is transforming the garden setting into a scene of harsh bleakness.

New developments are particularly damaging when they are out of scale, and the headquarters building for the Eagle Star Insurance Company towers over the town and ruins the views over a wide area, because of its sheer bulk and size. The headquarters of the Cheltenham and Gloucester Building Society in Clarence Street may not tower over· the town but its ludicrous swelling of the Regency idiom makes it a crass intruder on the Regency scene.

On the corner of Bayshill Road and St Georges Road two villas, the former Milverton and Pyatts hotels, have been amalgamated into a swollen and shapeless whole. A pair of villas at Nos. 113

55

and 115 Bath Road are empty and likely to be demolished unless the Council enforces a Repairs Notice. Montpellier Arcade, a handsome row of covered shops with a dignified stone entrance, stands empty. Several villas are now threatened by road proposals—Elmfield in Overton Road, Tower House in Prestbury Road and the Parabola Garage— and the continuity of the quiet residential street St Lukes Road is to be broken by a new road.

Cheltenham will continue to be damaged as long as offices continue to move into the centre of the town and the villas lose their residential character. The desertion of the squares near the town centre in preference for life in the surrounding Cotswold countryside is contributing to their decay.

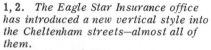

1, 2.   The Eagle Star Insurance office has introduced a new vertical style into the Cheltenham streets—almost all of them.
3.   The new High Street style.
4.   Portland Street car park, replaced Regency houses near the church.
5.   Headquarters of the Cheltenham and Gloucester in swollen Regency-modern.
6.   St Luke's Road, endangered by road proposals.
7.   Extending a Regency house.
8.   A pair of Regency villas in the Bath Road, threatened by offices.
9.   The car park replaced Edward Jenner's house in this terrace.
10. Montpellier Arcade, empty.

1

Chesterfield

Since 1204 Chesterfield has had as its centre a large open Market Place. In 1964 the councillors welcomed the proposals of the Hammersons property company which wanted to build a 5½-acre town centre development that would not only cover the whole Market Place but also obliterate the historic Low Pavement area. At the same time Lloyds Bank Consortium took charge of the redevelopment of the small-scale Shambles area on the east side of the Market Place. In April 1974 Hammersons announced that, because of 'the political uncertainty with which the property industry is confronted,' it had 'decided to defer any commitment or work on the Chesterfield central area scheme'. But the Council remains determined to push through this incredible scheme involving the total destruction of Chesterfield as a historic town. In February 1973 the Chairman of the Planning Committee said 'The Labour group intend to implement the policy approved by the Council and will brook no interference from those who dissent.' The guardians of the town are as determined to wreck the centre as they have been in the past to allow the destruction of so many buildings in other parts of the town.

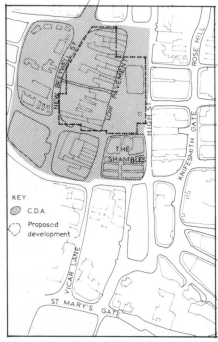

KEY:
C.D.A.
Proposed development

1. *East side of the Market Place. This range of buildings and the Shambles behind are threatened by the Lloyds Bank redevelopment.*
2. *South side of the Market Place. On the right, the fifteenth-century Peacock Inn, in the centre, the Market Hall. All are threatened by the Council/Hammerson redevelopment plans.*
3. *Fine early eighteenth century house in St Maryhill, derelict and abused by road signs.*
4. *Group of early nineteenth century houses standing marooned in a desert of demolition sites and road works.*
5. *Eighteenth-century houses on the south side of the Market Place.*

2

Edinburgh

The city of Edinburgh stood until the late eighteenth century perched in giddy isolation above moorland to the south and the Loch to the north. Within this city people worked and lived, crammed in towering tenements, noblemen, merchants and thieves, all using the same common stair. By the mid eighteenth century new ideas were in the air. The style of life dictated by the old town became intolerable to the richer, travelled citizen of Edinburgh. The result of this disaffection was the construction of Europe's most romantic classical town. After 1766 the First New Town was built, beyond the Loch, as a series of three parallel streets stretching between two large squares. All was rectilinear, controlled, classical. Here the rich merchant moved—to live without shop, tavern or markets, the life of classical dignity and repose. The expansion continued and by 1830 the First New Town was surrounded on all sides by later, more picturesque development. To the west were the crescents of the Moray Estate. A rigid grid of solid low terraces lay to the north while on the east there stretched out a more random grid behind Hillside Crescent. Meanwhile, Edinburgh had expanded to the south. At first development had been orderly, almost in competition with the New Town, but soon instead of classical terraces there began to rise acres and acres of vernacular tenements. This became Edinburgh's twilight city of the nineteenth century.

So Edinburgh is a city of contrasts. The most obvious is the physical difference between the spiky, tightly-packed network of the Old Town perched above and the cool classicism of the eighteenth-century New Town below. On another level the contrasts are equally striking. While the New Town preens its splen-

didly fashionable plumage the south side of the city, with its beautiful vernacular eighteenth-century tenements and formal terraces equal to any of those in the New Town, is blighted and rapidly succumbing to demolition. The villain in the past was the University of Edinburgh. Expanding within the CDA on the south side of the city, it demolished great chunks of the area including two sides of the 1760 George Square and the seventeenth-century tenements around Bristo Port. Now the Royal Infirmary is expanding, in the process demolishing early nineteenth century Lauriston Place. In place of these lovely houses which have some rare and remarkably elaborate interiors, the hospital will build an eight-storey block with a 55-metre chimney. The architect for the

1.   *1970s Edinburgh: the new St James's Centre dominates the city.*
2.   *The doomed north side of George Square.*
3.   *St Mary's Street, off the High Street, to go for a new road.*
4.   *Block of 1760 houses in George Square, to be demolished. In the background is the University's image of the new Edinburgh.*
5.   *Lauriston Place, early nineteenth century, now destroyed.*

hospital is Sir Robert Matthew, adviser on conservation in Scotland to the Secretary of State.

There are great contrasts too in the Corporation's own approach to conservation. The New Town is a Conservation Area and the city's special project for European Architectural Heritage Year. The Old Town, an essential foil to the New, is neither a Conservation Area nor a Heritage Year project. Instead it is split by the boundary of another of the city's Comprehensive Development Areas. This split will become a physical fact if the proposed relief road becomes a reality, breaking across the point where Canongate meets the High Street. The route of the road continues to the south from the Old Town, demolishing baronial-style tenements in St Mary's Street, to the Pleasance. This is the boundary of the Leonards CDA, a cleared wasteland below Arthur's Seat.

Even within the favoured New Town there are some extreme contrasts. While it contains the best preserved parts of Edinburgh it also contains the infamous St James's Centre—a mound of unspeakable ugliness. This commercial centre stands on the site of James Craig's 1779 St James's Square, on the eastern perimeter of the New Town. It was developed in 1963 by Ravenseft and the Corporation, and stands in awful isolation towering over Adam's famous and beautiful Register House, surrounded by clearance, waiting for the city to build its unlikely road scheme. The St James's Centre is only one of many new buildings in strident contrast with the character of the city. In Hanover Street, a group of 1760 houses has been demolished for offices and will be replaced by replicas.

Buildings are at risk throughout the city. The area around Adam's University in Nicholson Street lies largely derelict;

6.   *Wedge-shaped block in Leith Street, soon to go.*
7.   *1760 houses in Hanover Street, now demolished and replaced by a replica.*
8.   *Eighteenth-century tenements making way for the St James's Centre.*
9.   *Adam's Register House with the St James's Centre looming behind it.*
10.   *Tall, late eighteenth century tenements in Leith Walk—demolished while this book was at the printer's.*

high, early nineteenth century classical tenements are to be demolished. The fight to save the vernacular tenements in St Patrick's Square and Nicholson Street now seems lost: 'slum clearance' has won the day. The fight to save Buccleuch Street is definitely lost. The Corporation's Master of Works has decided that the buildings are dangerous and, though Listed, they are to be demolished.

Edinburgh's port at Leith is rapidly being eroded. Dock buildings and classical tenements are all being swept away by the Corporation for slum clearance. The fishermen's cottages in the High Street are now doomed.

11. *Lone survivor of 1779 St James's Square.*
12. *Derelict early nineteenth century tenements in Drummond Street.*
13. *Tenements in Nicholson Street: future uncertain.*
14. *Drummond Street tenements, detail.*
15. *Mid-eighteenth-century vernacular tenements in Buccleuch Street, declared dangerous by the City after 200 years.*

Frome

3

Frome was a medieval market town that grew to prosperity during the seventeenth and eighteenth centuries as a wool manufacturing town. Mills and homes for the mill owners and mill workers were built to the south and west of the town's medieval core. Frome prospered until the end of the eighteenth century, when the wool industry went into decline, so that in 1865 the last of the great mills, called Shepherds, closed down. This collapse in its prosperity had one redeeming feature: the physical character of the town escaped being torn apart by Victorian improvers. This meant that Frome survived until today as a unique early industrial town, complete with an area of seventeenth-century workers' cottages, on a medieval street pattern. It seems unlikely that Frome will survive the present-day spate of improve-

1. *Frome is unique in still retaining an area of workers' cottages dating from the seventeenth century, known as Trinity. It will be swept away as part of the Council's slum clearance policy, before any proposals have been made for a replacement.*
2. *Vallis Road is to be widened as part of the road plan. The 1697 terrace will be demolished.*
3, 4. *Seventeenth-century houses in Cork Street, 4, and early nineteenth century Monmouth House, 3, are all derelict. The owner has applied twice for Listed Building Consent to demolish.*
5. *Behind the Badcox Chapel this eighteenth-century house will go for a temporary car park.*
6. *Rook Street Chapel, 1707, remains derelict, although the exterior has been cleaned.*
7. *The seventeenth-century Sheppard's Barton off Catherine Hill, due to be demolished for slum clearance.*

KEY
Conservation Area
Widened roads
Proposed roads
1 The Trinity
2 Shepherds Barton
3 Catherine's Hill 5 Melrose House 7 Cork Street 9 Bath Street
4 Sun Street 6 Whittox Lane 8 King Street 10 Vallis Road

ments. The Council has little feeling for the historic nature of the town. It wants to clear the seventeenth-century cottage area, called The Trinity, and similar courts of cottages off Catherine's Hill. To a 'progressive' Council these appear as slums. To improve the traffic flow around the town, a ring road is being built through Frome's centre. In a town the size of Frome (population 13,900) this is a ludicrously destructive and expensive undertaking. It involves the destruction of much of the core it aims to protect. It goes through eighteenth-century houses at Sun Street, within inches of the fine Melrose House in Whittox Lane, and right on into the town centre. The new road has the approval of the Department of the Environment as far as the town centre. The second stage is more tricky. If built to link the centre to the A 362 it would involve the demolition of an eighteenth-century pub, the nineteenth-century Mechanics Institute and good eighteenth-century houses on the banks of the River Frome. On the southern side of the town the existing A 362 would have to be widened as a result of the construction of the ring road. This would involve amongst other things the demolition of a 1690s terrace in Vallis Road. Where the two sections of the ring road meet in the town centre there is, by strange coincidence, a large new commercial development in progress. It is being financed by Commercial Union Properties Ltd. The Town Council owns the land, and the scheme will provide 70,000 square feet of shopping space. This is the face of the new Frome. The character of the town is being eroded by a mass of smaller threats. The early 19th century Monmouth House and the gabled houses in Cork Street are rotting. All of them are Listed: their

8. *Badcox Chapel, 1825, in Catherine Street will be demolished for the temporary car park.*
9. *Sun Street is on the alignment of the new road. Both sides will be demolished.*
10. *Mechanics' Institute in North Parade, circa 1870, stands in the way of the new road.*
11. *Bath Street's nineteenth-century Gothic school, now derelict. To be demolished for a commercial development.*
12. *Early eighteenth century Iron Gates House in King Street is apparently doomed.*

owner has applied several times to demolish them and they remain derelict. The plans for pedestrianising Catherine's Hill will mean that a parallel street has to be cleared for servicing. An early nineteenth century Chapel in Catherine Street will go, together with a fine eighteenth-century house (both owned by the Council), to provide a temporary car park.

The Grade I Listed Iron Gates House in King Street is empty and the Historic Buildings Council has refused a grant. The Gothic-style school in Bath Street is derelict and threatened with demolition. Also in danger are the seventeenth-century houses at 4 and 5 Catherine Street, and Bridge House.

13. *Whittox Lane. This compact, winding street will become a part of the wide new relief road.*

Glasgow

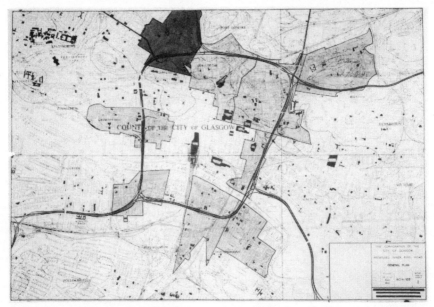

Map showing CDAs (grey) and proposed motorways.

'The sections of motorway through the heart of the city are generally of three or four lanes in each direction, with frequent flyover junctions. By 1976, when the whole length of the city is spanned from east to west by motorway, travelling time to Glasgow airport from the centre of Glasgow will be cut to half the present twenty minutes.' Thus Glasgow Corporation proudly advertises what 130 million pounds worth of expenditure on roads is achieving for the businessman who might be attracted to the city.

Once a medieval university city, Glasgow's great period of growth followed the Act of Union of 1707. Because of its strategic west coast position the city grew as trade expanded with the Colonies. In the early nineteenth century cotton replaced tobacco as the main import and, as Scottish coal was exploited heavy industries grew up along the Clyde. Each period of growth resulted in new buildings, and a rich mixture of old and new has until recently always been the result. Glasgow had a rich inheritance of buildings from all periods and it was possible to see and admire the way the city had grown.

Today the city behaves as though the past was only something to be ashamed of. It is not just Glasgow's appalling slums that have disappeared, it is the whole complexity of the city's evolution that has been ruthlessly destroyed. The massive motorway box has been used as a means of slum clearance but it has also blighted and caused the demolition of buildings of major importance. Two schools of international importance designed by Scotland's pioneer modern architect, Charles Rennie Mackintosh, the Martyr's School and the Scotland Street School, lie on the proposed route of the urban motorway. A perfect pair of neo-classical College residences designed by James Adam (Listed Grade A) have already been demolished to make way for the elevated section of the motorway that will replace the High Street and run within a few hundred feet of the Cathedral. The famous Tolbooth Tower will be skimmed by the same road and the Episcopalian Church of 1751 will have to be demolished, as will the magnificent rock-faced warehouses in Bell Street. Aided by current CDA legislation the City has been able to designate almost half the central area of the city for total redevelopment.

To the west of the High Street is the area known as the Merchant's City. More than anywhere else this area, in its scale, mixture and type of building, represents the old core of Glasgow and, like most small-scale city centres, it is under severe redevelopment pressure. Though it appears to be older, in

fact it dates from only 1751 when it was laid out by rich city merchants as a 'New Town'. But, not being under one overall contract, this New Town developed in a rather haphazard way.

During the nineteenth century most of the original buildings in the New Town were gradually replaced by offices and tobacco warehouses. But the grid pattern and scale were respected. The rich merchants, as their town became more commercial, moved west to the newer fashionable residential area. The quality of the area dropped and cheaper users moved in. By the end of the nineteenth century it had become the area of Glasgow's fruit and vegetable markets. Glasgow was now booming, but the city's commercial centre had moved west, so the old Merchant City escaped being totally

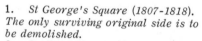

1. *St George's Square (1807-1818). The only surviving original side is to be demolished.*
2. *Scotland Street School, designed by Charles Rennie Mackintosh, on the route of the City's proposed urban motorway.*
3. *St Andrew's, Turnbull Street, built in 1751, is the oldest Episcopalian Church in Glasgow still in use. The motorway proposals would take its roof off as the road sails over it on stilts.*
4. *Virginia Place. Much of the disappearing Merchant City was of this style and design.*
5. *Bell Street warehouse—threatened by the motorway.*
6. *This terrace in the Merchant City (Wilson Street) may have been designed by the Adam brothers.*
7. *1820 terraced houses in West George Street, derelict and due for demolition.*
8. *1854 Venetian Eagle Buildings in Bothwell Street, to be demolished.*
9. *The expanding Art School will consume this 1830 tenement in Renfrew Street.*
10. *Elgin Street Congregational Church, at risk.*
11. *Greek Thomson's Caledonia Road Free Church, now only a shell, and the fact that it is likely to be surrounded by a new motorway makes it survival unlikely.*
12. *St Enoch's Station, 1880, now mostly used as a car park. The City and British Rail have expressed their intention of having it down.*

11

rebuilt to a larger scale by the late-Victorian commercial concerns. As a market and small-scale business area it has ticked over happily and usefully for a hundred years. But now, like most of the city, it is threatened by Glasgow's mania for large-scale redevelopment. Small businesses are being eased out and developers are amassing sites that can, because the city has abandoned plot ratio control, be rebuilt on a massive scale.

Large-scale redevelopment threatens Glasgow's other areas of homogeneous growth. The area to the west of the old city grew rapidly in the early nineteenth century as the city's new residential suburb. By 1860 a rigid grid of tenements and houses reached far west and was terminated by the austere classical crescents and terraces of the Park Hill estate. The speed of the city's commercial expansion, however, did not give this area a chance to mature. By 1840 a character change was in progress. Rebuilding began, replacing houses with offices, but mostly the relatively narrow domestic plots were adhered to. So this western area of Glasgow began to develop its characteristic narrow yet tall late-Victorian office blocks so reminiscent of the commercial areas of late nineteenth century American cities such as Chicago. Now in turn the twentieth century is eating at the fabric. But no longer are developments modest enough to keep to existing plots. Only whole blocks are good enough now.

13. *Greek Thomson built these tenements in the 1870s, now threatened.*
14. *Derelict nineteenth-century warehouses in James Watt Street.*
15. *Carlton Place, Lauriston. The John Knox Church, 1806, is being demolished.*
16. *More Greek Thomson tenements in the Gorbals, to be demolished.*

1

Gloucester

The destruction of Gloucester has been going on since the nineteenth century, but until recently its centre had all the qualities of a perfect medieval town. Narrow, winding streets full of half-timbered houses clustered around the soaring tower of the cathedral, the perfect setting for the cosy adventures of Beatrix Potter's Tailor of Gloucester. With its later, spacious College Green, a cathedral close that could have been the setting for one of Trollope's Barchester novels of clerical intrigue, Gloucester embodied the finest characteristics of an English cathedral town.

It is this large inheritance of medieval and post-medieval buildings that has been progressively sacked since the Second World War. Between 1949 and 1974 nearly 200 Listed buildings were demolished. A few steps away from the perfection of the Cathedral precincts the new Westgate demonstrates the official attitude to the historic centre of Gloucester. In this heart of the city no less than twenty-five Listed buildings were demolished for the Westgate Development. They have been replaced by council flats in a debased Festival of Britain style, painted in feeble colours,

4

an ignominious blot on the heart of the city.

The city authorities, blind to the tangled heritage of the ancient streets, determined to make the centre of Gloucester an effective regional shopping centre. This has led to a large influx of traffic into the heart of the city. The Eastgate shopping centre associated with the new King's Square has replaced a familiar mixture of old buildings, destroying the vernacular rhythm of the main street. There is an air of contemporary squalor about the scheme, partly generated by

the uniform nature of so many of the chain store shop fronts, the appearance of the utilitarian walkways and back elevations and the dreary sight of the fountains full of litter.

One of the amazing things about this city is the extraordinary neglect of the remains of the ancient Llanthony Priory, once among the richest in England. It lies now on land owned by the nation, in the shape of British Rail, and is a totally abandoned wreck lying among rubbish and weeds.

The whole site of the Priory should be

5

6

safeguarded. It remains astonishing that such an important part of a city's heritage should be so blatantly neglected. The current condition of Llantony Priory is a worrying sign of the attitudes towards the past in a city which has much to safeguard for the future.

Gloucester has an unexpected inheritance of nineteenth-century warehouse building, concentrated around the docks. These splendid tall brick buildings stand empty and derelict.

Roads and traffic have brought their inevitable toll of destruction to the city. New roads are worryingly close to the centre of the city and have already seriously affected the distant views of the Cathedral.

For a city of fairly modest size Gloucester has more than its fair share of redundant buildings. St Nicholas' Church stands empty and derelict: it is listed the same grade as Gloucester Cathedral. St Bartholomew's Almshouses, 18th-century Gothic in style, sit waiting for someone to decide whether or not a new use can be found for them.

It is pointless to dwell on the appalling losses that have occurred in this city but it is not too late to raise the mediocre standard and out-of-scale nature of the replacements. Much of the character of the medieval city has gone. There is a chance to save what is left of the Cathedral City but Gloucester is not far from being a Cathedral surrounded by an indifferent chain store shopping-scape.

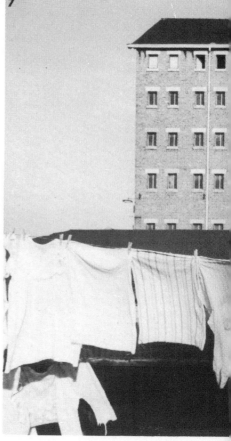

1. *The new ring road.*
2. *Llanthony Priory, used as a scrap merchant's dump.*
3. *Elizabethan farmhouse, on the same site and in similar condition.*
4. *Georgian Gothic St Bartholomew's Almshouses, empty and perilously close to the new road.*
5. *Bearland House stands empty in the centre of the city.*
6. *Bearland House, interior.*
7, 8. *Gloucester Docks. Magnificent stacks of warehouses by Telford, 1830s. The dock authority continues to press for permission to demolish.*
9. *St Nicholas' Church, late medieval, obsolete.*

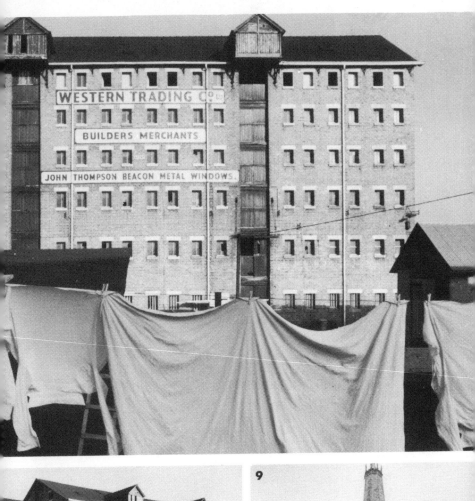

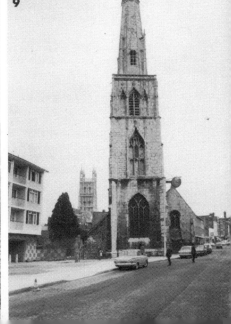

This Thames-side town still contains some evocative memories of its past as a prosperous port and fashionable middle-class resort (before the coming of the railway). But these remains, though startling in their quality, are now few in number. Gravesend suffered much in the war but has suffered more since.

The town was given a new civic centre in 1964 and demolitions have continued so that now practically the entire centre of the town has been cleared. The small-scale cobbled streets of central Gravesend now survive only as boundaries between fields of tarmac. All has been levelled to provide ample acres for the visiting motorist to park his car. The western side of this ravaged area is bordered by the High Street and the 1731 church. The contemporary rectory, owned by the Council, has been left to crumble.

On one side of the High Street is the early nineteenth century Doric portico of the Town Hall, now only a screen to a later market, while on the other stands a group of derelict early eighteenth century houses. These are of

immense architectural importance, not only because they represent the last remnant of the rebuilding of Gravesend after the fire of 1727, but also because they are of a type practically unique in England. They are timber-framed and clapper-board in the usual Kent vernacular way. But then, marvellously, they are dressed with ambitious classical decorations of pediments, architraves, and cornices. They have been allowed to stand empty for years. They are Listed, so the Council could have served a Repairs Notice, but it has preferred to negotiate and dither with the owner who has always wanted them down. Their final collapse can only be a matter of time.

1. *The centre of the town has literally become one gigantic car park.*
2. *The eighteenth-century rectory, owned by the Council. Soon it will fall.*
3,4. *Rare timber-framed, clapper-board houses in the High Street.*

Gravesend

4

Hereford

2

3

It is only recently that Hereford Council has realised the possibilities of comprehensive redevelopment and two large schemes have been under consideration for changing the face of the city. Despite having its major road plans implemented, Hereford still retains its medieval street pattern, but now the old city is threatened as never before. What has already been done serves to show in its small way how little is needed to upset the city's traditional character. As each building is destroyed, the remainder becomes more vulnerable; the plans on hand at the moment may be the turning point between keeping Hereford and losing it forever.

At the time of writing, approximately a third of the central area within the line of the city wall and the modern ring road is having plans prepared for comprehensive redevelopment. The northwest segment bounded by Eign Street, Newmarket Street and Widemarsh Street is the subject of a scheme approaching readiness in the offices of Pagebar Investments Ltd. This involves putting 218,000 square feet of shops, offices and car parking onto the $6\frac{1}{2}$-acre site.

The buildings are at present largely derelict and in need of development but the proposed scheme will be on a scale unprecedented in the city. Among the buildings involved are Bewell House, once the Master Brewer's House, which at present graces a car park, the old bowling green with its club house, and the west side of Widemarsh Street, where the Black Swan Hotel is already vacant. The whole side of this street forms a group covering a wide range of styles and periods and though some of the buildings will stay, others will be 'not retained' (i.e. destroyed), and the quality of the street will be lost. Another area, bounded by Widemarsh Street, Maylord Street, Commercial Street and High Town, a hollow square faced by many good buildings, is the location of a Taylor Woodrow/City consortium plan involving 60,000 square feet of shopping space and thousands of square feet of offices using powers of compulsory purchase. Perhaps the single saddest blow will be the dismantling of the covered Butter Market of 1861. These two developments would increase Hereford's shopping space by 330,000 square feet, whereas the Council's own shopping study revealed a need for only 50,000 square feet of new shops by 1981.

Hereford already bears many scars from the insensitive amalgamation of varied, small-scale units in the street frontage into long, characterless office facades. This is a less dramatic threat to the feeling of a town than the giant free-standing blocks of the comprehensive development, but gradually drains away the architectural and historic qualities of the town. The example of Littlewoods in High Town is heightened by the absurd sticking on of the facade of a timber-framed building with its roof gable emerging out of the roof slope of its parent like a dormer. Marks and Spencers provides a similar example, and the patterned life of the Victorian City Library's facade reproaches the featurelessness of its neighbours. A grossly insensitive ap-

1. *Late eighteenth century Bewell House awaits its fate in the hands of Pagebar Investments.*
2. *Drybridge House, severely neglected.*
3. *Eighteenth-century mansions in St Owen Street. The three-storeyed house at the right of the picture is to be replaced by the new Herefordshire Arts Theatre.*
4. *Widemarsh Street will be breached by the Pagebar development.*
5. *Littlewoods: joke conservation.*
6. *High Town, with the facade of the Butter Market.*
7. *The cast iron of the Butter Market in the old town is to be dismantled in Taylor Woodrow's commercial development, for partial re-erection elsewhere.*
8. *Taking the stuffing out of Barclay's Bank. Front of a grand eighteenth-century Inn.*

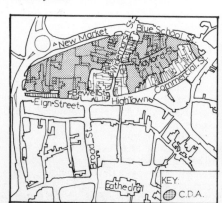

proach to the quality of the street is displayed in the crude breaking of the street line by the office development at 6 St Nicholas Street. Another more subtle form of attack is exemplified in the gutting of Barclays Bank by Alec French and Partners of Bristol—a nice way out of the embarrassment of owning a historic building. There is no sign that developments of these three kinds will not go on eating away at Hereford. Outstanding threats to individual buildings in Hereford include the planned removal of one of an uninterrupted run of grand eighteenth-century mansions in St Owen Street for the Herefordshire Arts Theatre. And finally there is Hereford's shame, Drybridge House, the first house you come to approaching the city from the south. Blighted by the new road behind, it was bought by the Council and has been neglected over the last five years. It was used to house problem families but it has deteriorated so rapidly that a Dangerous Structure Notice can be expected daily; it is unlikely to survive until the publication of this book.

9. *Broad Street. Nineteenth-century vigour gives way to twentieth-century blankness.*
10. *Square peg in a round hole: St Nicholas Street.*

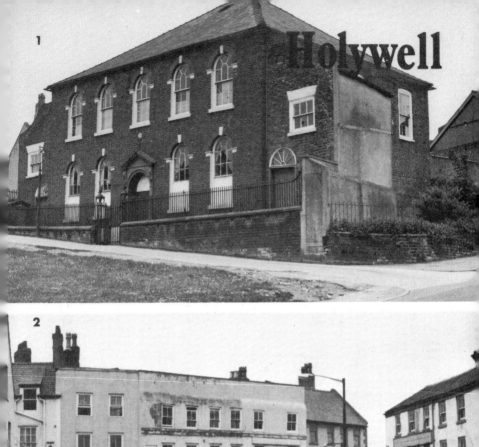

Holywell

4

Holywell in Flintshire, North Wales, has been a remarkably unspoilt hillside market town. Stucco-faced and brick two- or three-storey houses from the eighteenth and early nineteenth centuries line the main streets, and the town is completed by a Victorian Town Hall and an early nineteenth century Chapel. All this was intact, in some places showing signs of wear, until the local Council decided to redevelop. The first phase has already begun, and at the top of Chapel Hill, where part of a town recently stood, a notice adorns derelict ground covered with weeds, saying 'Town Centre Redevelopment Phase I: Residential Area'. There has been total clearance on one side of the hill and demolition of the parallel Well Street is well advanced. The handsome, red brick Chapel, Georgian in spirit, now stands in forlorn isolation on the wasteland. This development, in conjunction with a scheme to improve access to the High Street, is now poised to sweep

away the eighteenth-century houses that at present so effectively close the westward vista up the High Street. At the other end Bagillt Street curves off to the north: there has been clearance here already and Nos. 5 and 7, a late eighteenth century pair of three-storey houses with small early nineteenth century shop fronts, stand vacant nearing dereliction. So, while the rump of the High Street will remain, the town will be left crudely truncated. Further along the same road a fine mid-eighteenth-century town house now occupied by the Department of Employment is in poor condition and must be at risk. The next-door house with an early eighteenth century double front is being vandalised. Ironically while the Council was busy demolishing many good buildings it took the trouble to restore the early nineteenth century intimate cottage close of Panton Place for use as old peoples' homes. For this the town won a Civic Trust Award in 1970.

5

1.   *The classical Chapel in Well Street, derelict.*
2.   *Late eighteenth century houses closing the view up the High Street, to be demolished.*
3.   *Eighteenth-century vernacular at the top of Well Street, soon to go.*
4.   *Large mid-eighteenth-century house owned by the Department of Employment, slowly rotting.*
5.   *Eighteenth-century houses in Bagillt Street stand derelict.*

Huddersfield

Huddersfield today epitomises the redeveloped town. Its central area is
arbitrarily defined and throttled by a
wide ring road, and inside the ring 25
per cent of the commercial space
(160,000 square feet) has been rebuilt
since 1965. Another 75,000 square feet
of commercial space and 470,000 square
feet of offices is under construction.
This work has been carried out using
the CDA machinery and typical Council-
developer deals, usually called 'part-
nerships'. The Corporation, working
on the principle of clearing the oldest
building first, is for the moment tolera-
ting the existence of its fine Victorian
commercial centre, while it concentrates
on mopping up the old edges of the city.
One doomed bit of pre-nineteenth-cen-
tury Huddersfield is the Beast Market.
It is east of where the town's medieval
church stood and the street pattern
within the Beast Market area still reflects Huddersfield's medieval origins.
All this is now part of a CDA and the
buildings are blighted in readiness for

1. *Curtains for Huddersfield: view
from a Gothic window.*
2. *The doomed Beast Market area—
one of the last parts of the city to retain
a good mix of eighteenth- and nineteenth-
century buildings.*
3. *The new triumphal entry into
Huddersfield.*

2

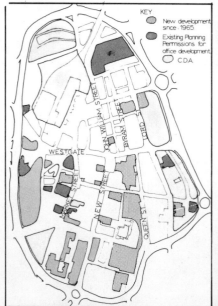

3

demolition. Surprisingly there is enough of old Huddersfield left for the Corporation to have declared four other large areas of the town CDAs. If everything goes according to plan by 1981 there will be hardly anything left in Huddersfield inside the ring road that was built before 1965. Outside the ring road the remnants of old Huddersfield look unlikely to last even until the 1980s. Leafy streets of late eighteenth century houses are being allowed to decay while nearby people are still living crammed into mean back-to-back houses.

4. *Early nineteenth century Cecil Street has considerable potential for rehabilitation, but is to be demolished.*
5. *Hammersons' shopping centre. Rain-stained concrete and bleak vistas are the new style for the city.*
6. *Developer's pretension on the rear elevation of the new Ravenseft shopping centre. What is it?*
7. *The Queen Hotel in Market Street, one of the few remaining early nineteenth century buildings in the centre, scheduled for redevelopment.*
8. *When the station is redeveloped the magnificent frontage onto St George's Square (1847, Pritchett) will be retained but the functional dignity of the railside warehouses will be lost.*
9. *Lion Buildings, built by Pritchett in 1854, recently Listed in an attempt to save it from a redevelopment threat.*

Hull

1

2

4

Hull is a maritime city that has fallen upon hard times. Its prosperity was based on its docks and its fishing industry. But now its inner docks are closed, fishing is no longer as prosperous as it was and Hull has not found itself a new economic base. Its central area steadily decays while the Council desperately looks for ways to inject new life into the city's economy. Land values are low, and the Council has declared much of Hull's Old Town a CDA: massive redevelopment seems imminent. But there is a lull. Pickings are more profitable elsewhere, and few developers are showing much interest in the town centre at the moment. However, when the Humber Bridge opens in 1976, Hull will suddenly become accessible to a much larger region. Then there will be a rush to develop and the chances are that precious little of Hull's old centre will survive.

The medieval town lies on a confined site between the Humber and the line of the old town docks which replaced the moats, curving round the north-east to the River Hull. From 1790 onwards a New Town, in the form of fine red brick terraces and stone public buildings, arose in the Albion Street-Jarratt Street-George Street area—to the north and beside the town docks and the River Hull. These new residential developments and the opening of the town docks in the late eighteenth and nineteenth centuries, changed the character of the medieval city. The expansion of commerce is especially noticeable in the warehouses on the High Street. The

1.   *View along Castle Street.*
2.   *The same view, with one side demolished and the other mutilated.*
3, 4.   *Before and after views of Hartley's warehouses in Railway Dock.*
5.   *Listed early eighteenth century houses in the High Street, in Corporation ownership, now derelict.*
6.   *Panelled interiors in the High Street ripped apart to provide firewood for tramps.*
7.   *What remains of Myton Gate is derelict and will soon be demolished.*
8.   *Looking south across the Prince Dock to the Humber Dock. The remnant of Jesse Hartley's Railway Dock can be seen in the centre.*
9.   *Myton Gate has been destroyed so that new life can flow back into the old town centre.*

Victorians and Edwardians completed the process with their administrative buildings. The modern development of the port along the Humber eventually superseded the old town docks. Already in the 1930s the Queen's Dock of 1775-8 was filled in and landscaped in a banal manner, becoming the present Queen's Gardens. A similar fate now hangs over at least part of the remaining splendid sequence of Humber Dock, Prince Dock and Railway Dock. The physical barrier of the town docks has in fact contributed to the decline of the medieval city since the war; the lack of access and the cramped site discouraged new businesses and the continuance of old ones. Only Whitefriargate and the market place function actively; otherwise many of the seventeenth- and eighteenth-century residential and nineteenth-century commercial buildings have fallen derelict. The existence of a redevelopment plan since 1954 (of which the CDA is a later part) has further run down the central area with planning blight. One facet of this plan is now reaching completion: the South Orbital Road is intended to improve east-west communications, alleviating the pressure of heavy dock traffic on the city centre and bringing new life to the Old Town. It has seriously affected the unity of the medieval city and its street pattern. Its construction has necessitated the demolition of the whole of the south side of Myton Gate, one of the ancient city streets, resulting in the loss of a number of seventeenth- and eighteenth-century houses and blighting in consequence the remaining north side, now directly threatened.

The future of the town docks, covering some thirty-five acres of central Hull, is a crucial planning and conservation issue. The dock walls and main warehouses are statutorily listed, but the condition of the latter may well provide

10. *The Market Place with King Street in the distance. The terrace on the right is under threat.*
11. *Arch in King Street leading to Prince Street.*
12, 13. *Wellington Street and Minerva Terrace. Modestly grand early nineteenth century sea captains' houses. The docks to which they related have gone, and the houses are derelict.*
14. *Rampant dereliction in Prince Street, owned by the Corporation.*

the excuse for their demolition. Jesse Hartley's great No. 7 Warehouse of 1845 was demolished for this reason by the Dock Board shortly before the Corporation took over responsibility. Hartley's massively impressive range by Railway Dock has already lost one section and the retention of the rest with the iron bridge over the dock entrance is essential to the scale and character of the dock complex. No. 6 Warehouse on the line of Castle Street and Myton Gate, though of smaller scale, plays an equally important role but is threatened by the South Orbital Road. The relation of the docks to the mix of terracing and warehousing in the Humber Dock Street—Wellington Street—Minerva Terrace area is also of great value.

Within the Old Town the toll of planning blight has been heavy. The north end of the High Street, outside the Conservation Area, contains fine mid-eighteenth-century houses (Nos. 195 to 202 owned by the Corporation) which are now terribly derelict and are still being vandalised. Prince Street with its subtle curve leading through under the King Street arch into the Market Place is a remarkable conception. The importance of its plan is recognised by the Corporation but it does not put an equally important emphasis on the buildings which gently follow the curve on the north side. The King Street elevation to the Market Place is to be restored but this will also involve the demolition of the north end. South of the Myton Gate/South Orbital dividing line, the whole of the Minerva Terrace-Wellington Street-Pier Street area is potentially at risk. Off Lowgate, No. 5 Scale Lane, a medieval jettied building, is now isolated on the edge of a new development replacing a bomb site. Many of the warehouses to the east side of the High Street are in a perilous state: the Pease Warehouses, 1743 and 1750-60, fronting the River Hull, are the earliest in the city and have deteriorated rapidly in Corporation ownership.

In the New Town a question mark hangs over the future of the Young People's Christian Institute on George Street. It incorporates two fine houses of c. 1790. The Institute is low on funds and would like to sell to a developer, and no doubt this would entail an application for Listed Building Consent to demolish. In the nearby Kingston Square, the Corporation has insisted on the retention of the

facade of Abraham's c. 1820 Greek Revival Medical School, but the proposed redevelopment involves the demolition of the adjoining houses.

The late eighteenth century pedimented block on Worship Street, closing the vista of Albion Street/Jarratt Street, is to be demolished. The Church Institute at the west end of Albion Street is empty.

Developers likely to be looking forward to 1976 include Ravenseft, involved in Hull for twenty years and with the demolition of the Infirmary among its achievements. Telegraph Properties and Intertown Estates are on Lowgate. Centrovincial Properties is involved in the Kingston Square scheme. Yorkshire and Lincolnshire Development Ltd is a new local firm with its eyes set on the pro-

15

posed Orbital Centre and is also completing an office block on George Street next to the Young People's Christian Institute.

15. *The Pease Warehouse, 1743, derelict and owned by the Corporation.*
16. *The pedimented block in Worship Street is to go.*
17. *Kingston Square. Only the facade of the old Medical School will be kept.*
18. *The Young People's Christian Institute. The owners want to sell this 1790 house to developers.*
19. *Threatened medieval remnant in Scale Street.*

King's Lynn

In many ways King's Lynn seems to be the essence of the English market town, the warm-hearted centre of the East Anglian plains. Now designated a town that should expand to absorb some of London's postwar overspill population, it has had to cope with all the problems and some of the benefits that go with a large and sudden increase in population. Lynn has always been a shopping centre for a wide area. It also maintains a high level of activity in the surprisingly busy port. It is then an active and prosperous centre of a wide region and a natural growth centre for the region. It is this growth that has put an impossible strain on the medieval fabric of the town centre, a strain that is beginning to crack the ancient heart of one of East Anglia's finest towns.

The Town Development Plan (1962), primarily an expansionist instrument, had two main objectives. It wanted a greatly increased amount of shopping in the town centre and at the same time more pro-

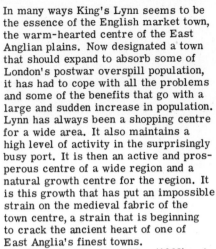

tection and enhancement of the historic core—which became a Heritage Area. (Heritage Areas were the predecessors of Conservation Areas.) A conflict of interests was inevitable. This conflict is made explicit in the new shopping precinct, which bears the name The Vancouver Centre. The interesting house where Captain Vancouver was born—an important place in the social history of the town - was demolished for the construction of the Centre. A few years earlier the house where Dr Burney and his daughter Fanny Burney lived was also destroyed. The designation of the historic streets King Street, Queen Street, Nelson Street and the Tuesday and Saturday Market Places as a Special Heritage Area is of doubtful value. It does protect the most obvious places that only a rank philistine could actually want to destroy, but has left the rest of the town open to serious losses.

Within King's Lynn's Heritage Area threats remain. There is a plan for King's Staithe Lane, running from South Quay to Queen Street, to be widened to provide access from the proposed relief road on the quay to the town centre car parks. This may never happen, but the uncertainty has already blighted the south side range of sixteenth-century buildings. If the relief road is built on the South Quay the traditional focus of the town where the timber and grain ships still call will be cut off by traffic. The warehouses and granaries are under-used at present and they have a very uncertain future. Bowker's Granary, a good-quality early nineteenth century brick warehouse, is now in a state of decay, undoubtedly a building of the greatest character.

For a town of its size Lynn has made some massive changes in its street pattern. Following the fashion, the Council is pedestrianising the High Street at the expense of the destruction of numbers of old streets behind for car parking and rear access. Tuesday Market Place itself is to be changed from a car park to a landscaped meeting place as the town's contribution to Architectural Heritage Year, but this could involve demolitions for an access road from the east. The revised List, published by the Department of the Environment in 1972, is now well out of date as the demolitions continue. Austin House, Norfolk Street and All Saints Street have all suffered and many good old houses are now derelict and 'ripe for redevelopment'. Some of these houses are silently awaiting the results of inquiries into their futures. Time is not on the side of empty property; decay soon starts and dereliction follows. No. 1 Stonegate Street, with Nos. 9 and 10, is likely to be the subject of a major redevelopment scheme. No. 42 Chapel Street, an eighteenth-century facade on an earlier building, belonging to the Council, has suffered neglect for years. With the houses that run on that side of the street (Nos. 16-24, a typical mansard-roofed block once common in the lesser streets of Lynn), it will be replaced by offices. The most one can hope for is the retention of the facade of No. 42 on the front of a new building—a very poor substitute for preserving the building.

Road proposals in Lynn as elsewhere are a major threat to historic buildings, and the sheer weight of traffic that is generated by the new roads causes severe damage and blight. The late eighteenth century Nos. 4 and 6 Littleport Street to the east of the town are in the line of a radial road to the bypass. Houses at 22 and 24 Gayton Road, Gaywood, built in 1693, are blighted by road plans, as is the attractive school of 1894. If these plans are carried out the sixteenth-century Bishop's Terrace will be damaged by the effects of traffic. Another kind of blight that is affecting parts of the town is official procrastination. Pilot Street, once scheduled for office development and now for housing, stands largely uninhabited and decaying. Similarly the officials seem uncertain what to do with the fine seventeenth- and eighteenth-century houses at 12-17 Southgate Street. Before the changes in local government structure a plan existed to turn them into old peoples' homes. It is not clear whether the new Council will continue with the scheme.

Lynn is still very vulnerable to neglect, roads, and selective conservation. The new local authorities must not sacrifice any more of the town's fabric while sitting back in their offices complacently admiring the 'heritage' area.

1. *Nos. 12-17 Southgate Street, condemned and decaying for years.*
2. *King's Staithe Lane, threatened by long-standing road proposals.*
3. *Bowker's Granary. A public inquiry is shortly to decide its fate.*
4. *No. 1 Stonegate Street, wanted for a new hotel.*
5. *The Vancouver Centre, named after a historic house which fell in its path.*
6. *Pilot Street, a delightful enclave on the brink of redevelopment.*
7. *Nos. 4 and 6 Littleport Street, blighted by the town's road proposals, now a background to a road sign.*
8. *Nos. 22 and 24 Gayton Road: wanted for a new road.*
9. *No. 42 Chapel Street, threatens the progress of an office block.*

Leeds

The largest town in West Yorkshire, Leeds has to face considerable pressures to redevelop, and it is far from certain that there is sufficient appreciation of her tough Victorian heritage to ensure that the real quality of Leeds will survive. The obvious monumental buildings like the Town Hall by Brodrick (1853-58) are cleaned up and cared for but the solid Victorian dignity of the commercial areas has already suffered considerable losses. Good buildings by Scott and Waterhouse in the Park Row area have gone and the future of several others lies in the balance.

But Leeds is not simply a Victorian city. Typically, like the High Street of any Yorkshire market town, the Briggate links up with parallel streets by lanes and courts. These were enhanced by the Victorians who saw their value and turned them into high, galleried, richly-decorated cast iron and glass arcades. Briggate in the eighteenth century assumed a certain Baroque dignity suitable for a prosperous commercial town. The

1. *Eighteenth-century houses in Briggate, all to be demolished by Metropolitan Estates and Property Company.*
2. *A lane off Briggate containing apparently the remains of a jettied timber-framed house. Several lanes like this were demolished in the MEPC scheme.*
3. *Victorian arcades, off Briggate, following the medieval lane system: creative building on the past.*
4. *Victorian commercial buildings in Boar Lane. All will go if the MEPC development goes ahead.*

113

little of this that survived the Victorian growth is now threatened by the crude proposals of the Metropolitan Estates and Property Company, which has already replaced medieval lane patterns in Briggate with a huge hole. Its proposals threaten an area bounded by Briggate, North Station Street, the railway and Boar Lane.

Boar Lane has a marvellous unity of Victorian buildings leading in a serpentine curve from the City Square to the splendid elliptical Corn Exchange (at present looking for a new use). The buildings on the south side of the street are Listed: they form a magnificent

115

street, with individual buildings varying from narrow Venetian facades to huge blocks of Victorian chambers. A walk down Boar Lane shows at once how the street, every time it changes direction, focuses on the right building. Particularly good is the striking view of Holy Trinity church (by Halfpenny, 1722-27). The result of an inquiry is pending but the street itself is almost derelict, a victim of planning blight.

Leeds went to enormous expense and trouble to pedestrianise the shopping area, and it became possible to appreciate the Victorian architecture without an accompaniment of traffic and fumes. However, no sooner was the pedestrianisation complete than the Victorian buildings began coming down. The construction of the ring road sliced the city up, isolating the centre from its suburbs. Just inside the ring road is Scott's General Infirmary (1862-68), for which Listed Building Consent for gutting is

being sought. The University in Leeds has spread in giant concrete fashion into the pleasant late Georgian and Victorian suburbs. It is certain that, however impressive the new buildings in Leeds may appear on the drawing boards of their commercial architects, they will fail to live up to the essential character of this remarkable city.

5. *View from Boar Lane across a newly-created hole to pedestrianised Headrow.*
6. *A rotting Georgian house with insensitive new University buildings muscling up behind it.*
7. *Part of the CDA already cleared by MEPC, looking towards Briggate.*
8, 9. *Decaying early nineteenth century buildings around the Corn Exchange.*
10. *A wing of Gilbert Scott's Gothic General Infirmary. Permission has been sought for gutting.*

Lincoln

A lot of Roman remains have been uncovered in Lincoln in the last few years. But then there has been a lot of opportunity as large areas of this historic city have been cleared for massive commercial and municipal redevelopment. Until Democratic Labour won control of the local authority in 1974 the entire city of Lincoln had been a pawn of the party politicians on the Council. Both Tory and Labour councillors backed the proposal for a destructive ring road and favoured deals with large development companies that brought some destructive redevelopments and threatened many more. A new ring road has been planned that would cut across the High Street and sever the medieval hill town from the rest of the city. Democratic Labour has promised to kill the plan, though it has not yet been removed from the books. Meanwhile large areas of the city

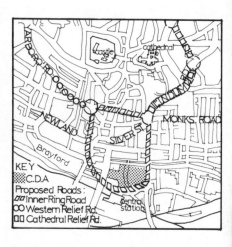

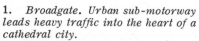

1. *Broadgate. Urban sub-motorway leads heavy traffic into the heart of a cathedral city.*
2. *Roman remains revealed, by-product of massive demolitions in the centre.*
3. *The proposed ring road crashes through this alley and across the High Street, breaking away the commercial city from the medieval hill town.*
4. *The Cathedral Relief Road will sweep away this early nineteenth century house.*
5. *Mid-eighteenth-century house in the High Street, in the path of the road.*
6. *Listed early eighteenth century house near the Cathedral, to be demolished.*

7

remain blighted and subject to progressive physical decay. Democratic Labour remains committed to a plan for a 'Cathedral Relief Road'. The City's dock area, Brayford, has been devastated —whole groups of listed warehouses were demolished to be replaced by two giant office developments, each giving about 120,000 square feet of offices. On the eastern side of Brayford, Woolco, a Woolworth's offshoot, was given permission to build a hypermarket (120,000 square feet) on land owned by British Rail. The new Council has rescinded this permission, because it would have killed the existing shops in the city centre. Objections from British Rail could lead to a public inquiry at which British Rail's case could be upheld. The Rail Board also wants to redevelop the Central Station site. Lincoln's market area has been declared a CDA and in consequence has become derelict. Within the CDA a street of eighteenth-

century cottages, Sincil Street, was compulsorily purchased by the Council for redevelopment, though for the time being a redevelopment deal with Town and City Properties is off. But none of these threats can be seen as past: Democratic Labour has only to be toppled and they will all be revived. The future of one of the country's greatest historic cities is at the mercy of a game of chance.

7. *Brayford Basin. Listed warehouses stood where the office block is now being built.*
8. *Cottages in Sincil Street, saved for the time being by the abandonment of the market CDA.*

Liverpool

Central Liverpool is still the supreme example of a Victorian commercial city. Its character comes as much from the miraculously preserved humble details— cut glass shop fronts, fancy lettering, Baroque gin palaces, cobbles and bollards —as from the large, richly-textured offices and chambers. This is just one facet of Liverpool's character: its history and traditional industry—docks and trade—have also left their mark on the city.

Liverpool grew inland from the peninsula between the River Mersey and the Pool of Liverpool. Canning Place now stands on the site of this tidal creek. The original seven streets of the town survive as Dale and Water Streets, Tithe Barn Street, Chapel Street, Old Hall Street, Exchange Flag, High Street and Castle Street. Within these streets the Victorians developed their commercial centre using the medieval street pattern as the basis for their imposing facades. This combination of medieval and Victorian is especially striking between Tithe Barn Street and Dale Street. It is precisely this area that the city has designated a CDA.

It was not until 1699 that Liverpool reached even Parish status, but after that things began to move fast. The Mersey brought in large ships bringing sugar, tobacco, cotton and so forth from Virginia and the West Indies. In 1709 the first dock was built on the creek in Canning Place. The town grew steadily until 1780, when there was a sudden burst of activity. By 1840 Liverpool had built itself a new town of regular red brick terraces complete with

1.　*Nile Street, in the New Town.*
2.　*The Dale Street frontage of the CDA.*
3.　*The Main Bridewell—within the CDA.*
4.　*The Tithe Barn Street edge of the CDA.*
5.　*Canning Place. 1830 stone-faced classical buildings backing onto a functional and simple warehouse emphasise how close the relationship between the docks and the rest of the city was. The block is now derelict.*
6.　*Detail of a derelict building in Canning Place.*

churches, halls and public rooms. Simultaneous with this growth south of the old town was the growth of the docks. By the end of the nineteenth century the docks had expanded both north and south of the old core and the city had sprawled inland, swamping the surrounding villages with small back-to-back terraces. As early as 1914 the first dock developments like Albert Dock were proving too small for the larger ships and they were becoming obsolescent. This was the beginning of the decline of the docks to the south of the city centre, a decline that has continued until today, leaving the city with acres of redundant docks, dock buildings and basins. All still belong to the Mersey Docks and Harbour Board who are uncertain what to do with them. The City Corporation has produced a draft plan but lacks the resources to purchase the Dock areas. Surprisingly at present no private developers are showing their predictably avid interest: presumably pickings are more profitable in other parts of the city. During the office boom of the mid-1960s Harry Hyams proposed the demolition of Jesse Hartley's 1840 Albert Dock for 11 million square feet of offices. The City thought that this was overdoing it a bit and suggested that 7 million square feet would fit more easily onto the site. Luckily Hyams could not raise the cash for his grandiose scheme and so the docks still survive. They are deserted and rotting although there is now a definite will to save them. Liverpool Polytechnic wants to take them over but has so far been unable to raise the money.

Other parts of the city did not escape the office boom. The Corporation designated Old Hall Street an office

7.   One of the later basins south of the Albert Dock. All are now obsolete.
8   The Chapel Walks area. All is total dereliction in the shadow of the plans for the new law courts.
9.   Nile Street, not on the route of the ring road, but still blighted by it.
10.   Jesse Hartley's Albert Dock, one of the supreme manifestations of the early nineteenth century's functional aesthetic.

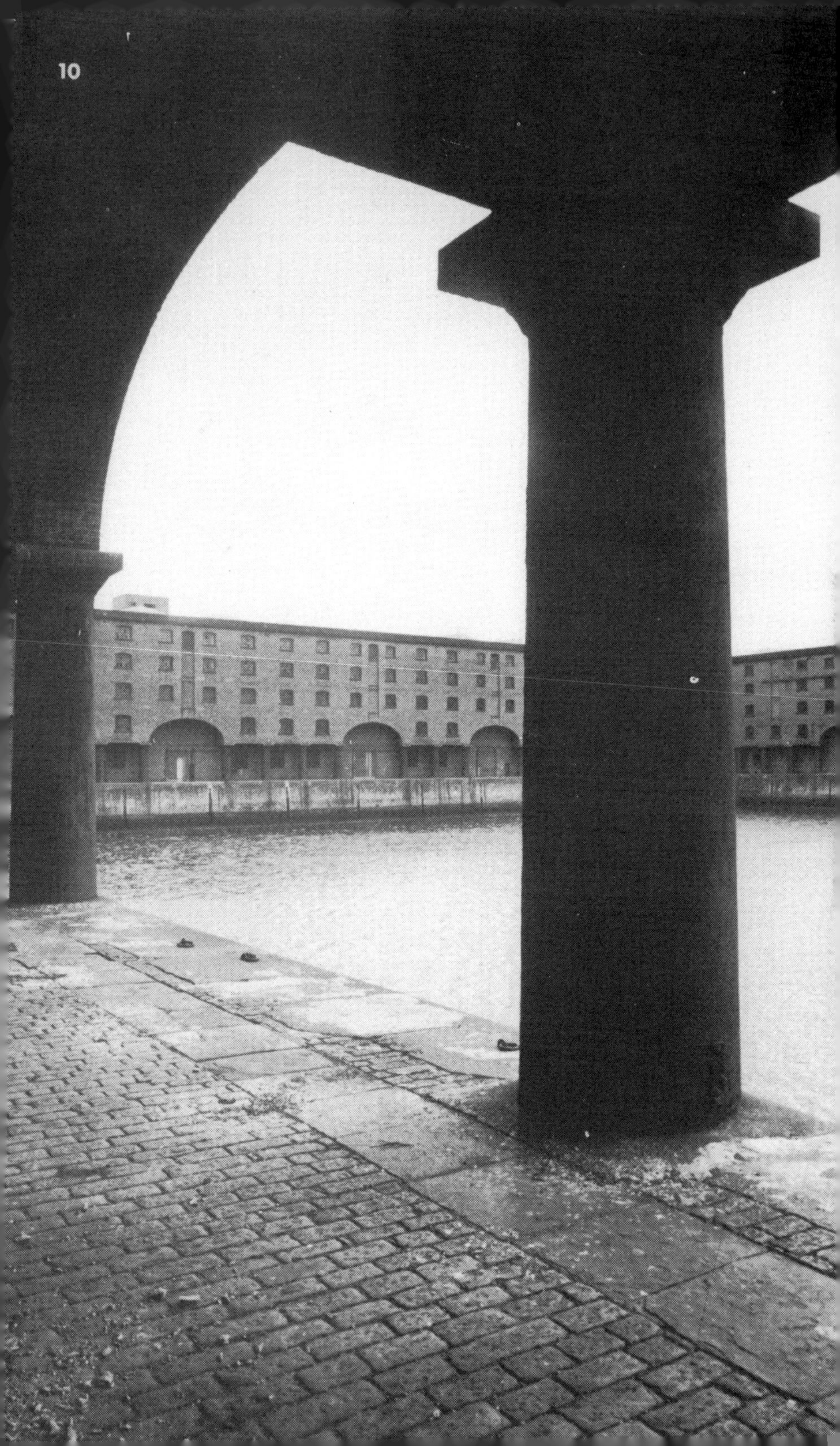
10

development area—and so it now is. 'Moorfields CDA' is the new name for the heart of the old city. Typically, since being declared a CDA ten years ago, the area has rotted and has fallen victim to piecemeal demolition. The Chapel Walks area, a collection of small-scale streets and warehouses originally designed to serve the now obsolete docks, is to be redeveloped by the City for its new law courts. It is sad that modern expressions of civic pride find it necessary not only to destroy existing buildings but also to obliterate entire areas, and destroy all the memorials of the past.

The area of Liverpool that is suffering most is the Georgian New Town. This area fell from fashion as the docks expanded and overshadowed the once middle class homes, so the decay began a long time ago. The City, rather than recognise the importance of the area and do something to stop the rot, has added to the blight by deciding to cut the ring road through the centre of the Georgian town. The road will go down Upper Parliament Street before ploughing through Great George Street and across Duke Street to Seymour Street and the London road. The mere existence of this proposal has been as destructive as the road itself would be. On the route of the road houses lie derelict, but dereliction is contagious and now whole streets not threatened by the road are boarded up. The rot has especially hit the area beneath the Anglican Cathedral. Here again, Liverpool seems content to wipe out a whole phase of its history, and this will be a tragedy not just because the Georgian town is good in itself, but also because Liverpool is a city of contrasts and mixtures. With the Georgian area gone, the whole city will be the less.

11, 12. *Duke Street. Eighteenth-century houses standing on the route of the ring road.*
13. *Seymour Street. Fine early nine-teenth century houses in the path of the ring road.*

More of the City of London stands devastated or is doomed now than was destroyed during the Blitz of 1941. It is true that the city has a habit of being destroyed. After the fire of 1666 it was quickly rebuilt. The Victorians and Edwardians replaced modest Georgian warehouses, offices and homes with splendid Baroque commercial palaces, when London was the commercial and shipping capital of the world. Their rich legacy was diluted by the bombing, but that was as nothing to what we are seeing now. Never since the Great Fire has so much of the City been destroyed so fast. And never before has the re-development so blatantly ignored the city's traditional scale and character. Even the most ambitious Victorian speculators built their commercial blocks with a respect for the City's street pattern—which was a legacy of the pre 1660s city—and built street architecture on a human scale. Now, the expansionist mentality of modern commercial enterprises results in the amassing of small-scale plots and the obliteration of the City's intricate medieval alley network, while massive new concrete and glass air-conditioned offices tower skywards, shattering the intelligible and familiar human environment of street surroundings. Development has run away with itself. There are now 48,200,000 square feet of offices in the City (half-a-million square feet of which is always empty) and applications still roll in.

To speed on the reconstruction of the City after the war, the government offered certain incentives to attract private capital to invest in building operations. For example it allowed an automatic 10 per cent increase of floor space in any new development. This worked, and private capital, and the speculators, were attracted. But having reconstructed, and tasted the profits, the beast wanted more. And the only way to get more has been to create new sites to reconstruct.

The City Corporation, during this continued rape, has shown itself unwilling rather than unable to call a halt. But, since it is largely made up of city businessmen it is presumably too much to expect it to value the fabric and structure of its City above the value of it as a viable building site. In fact, the City Corporation has been busily des-

troying whole areas of the city along with the worst of the developers.

It was the Corporation that decided to build the major east-west road along the River Thames. Where stood Georgian and Victorian pubs, warehouses and terraces, is now nothing but a wide road with an elevated access to Queen Victoria Street which wraps round Wren's St Benet, Paul's Wharf. The fabulous remains of Baynard's Castle were briefly uncovered during the summer of 1973. They are now buried again, but this time beneath concrete. Piles for the road have been driven

1.   St Benet, Paul's Wharf, surrounded by swirling concrete roads that have also swept away practically the whole of the city's riverside.
2.   Billingsgate Market, to go the way of the Coal Exchange, the Stock Exchange, and other Victorian halls of commerce.
3.   Christ Church, Newgate Street. The noble shell of one of Wren's largest churches, built on medieval foundations, mutilated by the City Corporation for a new road in 1973, while a site opposite lay vacant.
4.   Lovat Lane, to disappear with the redevelopment of Billingsgate.
5.   The site of a block of Victorian buildings fronting Martin Lane and Laurence Pountney Lane. The Victorian rebuilding of a Wren tower in Martin Lane goes next.

through part of the castle; the rest will
be covered by Post Office extensions.
The riverside buildings that were not
actually demolished for the road were
made 'ready for development' by it.
Queenhithe, the last working dock in the
city, was demolished in 1971 for a hotel.
It was the Corporation that demanded
the demolition of Bunning's unique Coal
Exchange, one of the earliest cast iron
structures in the world, pre-dating the
Crystal Palace. The City wanted it for
road widening, but the site is unused
after ten years. It was the City which
demolished the late Georgian houses in
front of the Guildhall and has now created
an ugly open space lined with large
concrete mushrooms. And it was the
City that destroyed, despite great public
opposition, the superb Baroque east
front of Wren's Christ Church, Newgate
Street, for a minor road improvement.
St James Garlickhythe has had its skin
of small houses peeled away from it as
part of the riverside road improvement.
Hardly the way to treat Wren's finest
monuments in the 250th anniversary of
his death.

When the Corporation has not been raping
the City itself, it has not hesitated to
allow others to do it. Angel Court, one
of the best examples of Georgian and
Victorian rebuilding on a medieval street
pattern, is now a huge hole in the ground.
Racquet Court, one of the only surviving
courts off Fleet Street, and containing
seventeenth-century houses, was totally
destroyed by Beaverbrook Newspapers'
extensions.

The pressures for redevelopment from
the Corporation, eminent commercial
organisations, and speculative developers, increase. Billingsgate Market
has now become an awkward block in
the riverside motorway route. The
Victorian market buildings, and the
narrow streets and alleys leading north
from Lower Thames Street to Eastcheap,
will go. In the place of the market
building will be a new market and office
block designed by R. Seifert. The Victorian offices that stretched west from
Martin Lane to Laurence Pountney
Lane have been demolished. And now
the Victorian rebuilding of a Wren
tower, on the east side of Martin Lane,
is also to be demolished. A huge tri-
angular block of Edwardian city chambers bounded by Old Broad Street and
Threadneedle Street is to be demolished

6. *The threatened City of London Boys'
School, Edwardian Baroque landmark on
the Thames.*
7. *The early nineteenth century
Bridewell Institute in Blackfriars,
derelict and threatened.*
8. *Victorian blocks in Queen Victoria
Street and Bucklersbury, to be demolished
and replaced by a fifteen-storey tower.*
9. *The City Club, built in 1833 by Philip
Hardwick, to make way for National
Westminster's 600-foot office tower.*

130

by the National Westminster Bank. In a marvellous way, when they rebuilt this block, they incorporated the old lane system as a series of internal, but public corridors. These lead to an internal courtyard in which stands a supreme example of early nineteenth century Greek Revival architecture. Philip Hardwick's City Club, of immense architectural importance, will not be spared.

A major landmark on the river front, the palace-like City of London Boys' School, built in 1881, is to be gutted by the Corporation, and round the corner in New Bridge Street the early nineteenth century Bridewell Institute has been empty for years, awaiting the granting of Listed Building Consent. Three late-Victorian wedge-shaped blocks opposite the Mansion House and bounded by Poultry, Queen Victoria Street and Bucklersbury, including some of the best and most prominent Victorian street architecture in the city, have been due for demolition since 1964, to be replaced by a fifteen-storey office block. The Salters Company wants to redevelop the eighteenth- and nineteenth-century buildings in Bow Lane, Watling Street and Watling Court. These streets form a Conservation Area and represent the last small-scale area in the centre of the City. While their future is decided, the buildings stand empty and decaying.

In the east of the City more monuments are due to go. Liverpool Street Station is to be redeveloped by British Rail. The train shed (the early part of which dates from 1874), with its huge pointed central span, tall cast iron arcade, crossing and transept, is a stupendous cathedral of the railway age. The DOE say it is not 'special' enough to be put on the statutory List of protected historic buildings. One can only conclude from this extraordinary statement (all similar stations of this age and quality were Listed long ago) that the DOE must have come to some arrangement with British Rail. The late eighteenth century East India Company's Cutler Street warehouses off Bishopsgate were the first large-scale response to the boom in London's trade that was to make it the commercial capital of the world—before the building of the enclosed docks. As such they are a historic monument of major importance, as well as being architecturally breathtaking. English

and Continental Properties have applied for permission to demolish them.

If great monuments like these have no future, there can be little hope for subtle, yet evocative remnants like the Circus by the Tower. Built by George Dance in the 1770s, the Circus was part of a romantic sequence. A square led to a crescent and then to the Circus. The site of the Circus is now wanted by the Corporation—for another road.

10. *St Paul's from threatened Bow Lane, one of the last small-scale streets in the City.*
11. *Eighteenth- and nineteenth-century houses in Bow Lane—empty for four years.*
12. *Round the corner from Bow Lane is Watling Court, also threatened.*
13. *Liverpool Street Station, cast iron cathedral of the railway age, to be destroyed by British Rail and replaced with 1,200,000 square feet of offices.*

London-Soho

Soho is the sort of centre that every city should have. The fact that it survives in London, surrounded on all sides by expensive office developments or potential redevelopment areas, is a miracle. It is important to realise the fragile nature of this miracle. Soho is under ever-increasing pressure from its surroundings. It could either become a part of Mayfair or Oxford Street, or suffer the kind of planned death that has afflicted Covent Garden.

If all the schemes now proposed come to pass, then Soho, the throbbing heart of London, will become the all-too-familiar dead city centre. Every time a community shop like a butcher's or a button maker's is replaced by an office

block or an exclusive cinema, Soho's pulse weakens.

To understand the subtle systems that make Soho work one has to look at its origins. It was a field on the perimeter of London until the late seventeenth century when Soho Square was laid out, south of the Oxford Road, as a fashionable residential area. Formal streets radiated from the Square, and it looked as though Soho was all set for the standard grid pattern of development, but this did not happen. The success of Soho Square encouraged speculative builders to try their luck in the area. Land which was mostly held as small individual freeholds was parcelled into building lots and leased out to the builders. So it grew without coordination, the landowners having in common only a shared determination to exploit their holdings. Soho then developed as a network of alleys, courts and lanes. By the end of the eighteenth century any formality promised by the original development was forever lost. In the eighteenth century Soho was the home of both French immigrants and a general mix of London shopkeepers, tradesmen and

modest merchants. The houses, except for some around the squares, were not grand and many were not even fashionable. Soho was a backwater even during the nineteenth century and largely escaped the development going on all round it. Regent Street was cut along its west side in the 1820s, and Shaftesbury Avenue and Charing Cross Road defined it to the south and east when they were constructed in the 1870s. The site of Soho's slums are marked today by the positions of the various nineteenth-century tenement blocks. Sandringham West now stands on the site of Newport Market, demolished when the new roads were cut. Others are Archer Street Chambers and St James's Dwellings. The unfashionable, seedy and vaguely insalubrious reputation of Soho kept it free from property speculators even in the early twentieth century.

In the 1950s Soho's reputation as a vice centre grew, but in the main people still came to shop, eat or drink, or just simply to escape from the big store atmosphere of west-end London. By the early 1960s the edges of Soho had started to go and sites in its centre were being amassed by developers so that when the property boom got going in the late 1960s, Soho's long-standing guardian—its seedy reputation—worked against it. Whereas in the past speculators merely reckoned this seediness would make it difficult for them to get a good rent for their development, the new brand of 60s developer simply saw seediness equalling low land values. In the boom of the late 60s, a development anywhere—even in seedy Soho—could not fail.

Since then eighteenth-century courts, streets, and blocks have been demolished like never before. And, more important for Soho's character, small businesses and traders have been edged out by increasing rents. Since it was proved in the 60s that Soho was a profitable place in which to speculate, all with the means have had a go. The Sutton Settled Estate which has owned a great lump of Soho for 250 years has, for 245 years, been content to accept low rents in return for low maintenance costs; now it has joined in the developing game. Where it cannot get permission to demolish, it rehabilitates to make expensive offices or flats. Both are disastrous for the local tradesmen who, once displaced, cannot afford to go back.

The situation now is desperate. Although
the development boom is over the
speculators will not abandon their investments or long-term plans. And the
easiest way to further their schemes at
present is for the developers to do
nothing. Soho is being deliberately run
down by the property companies who
now own so much of it. This is an excellent way of getting rid of inconvenient
Listed buildings. It is no coincidence
that most of Soho's empty buildings are
within its Conservation Area. Westminster City Council has not only done
nothing significant to stop this decay; it
has actually contributed to it itself.
The Sandringham West tenements were
emptied of their Council tenants for a
massive office and luxury flat development. Immediately the flats were emptied Westminster moved in and smashed
all the plumbing—a hasty move for, after
a stirring campaign, an action group
forced Westminster to keep the tenements. They are now being rehabilitated
by the Council. The survival of Westminster's outdated road plan has also
assisted the process. The old road-
widening line on many of the roads still
has to be conformed to by any new
development, with destructive effects
on, for instance, Wardour Street and
Broadwick Street.

Westminster's Conservation Area covers
only a quarter of Soho. Obviously it is a
shallow gesture, but even if Westminster
were to fight hard to conserve the fabric
of the area this would be no guarantee
that Soho would survive. An expensively

1.   *Richmond Buildings, built in 1732,
demolished by Westminster City Council
as slums. The site is now a car park.*
2.   *Early eighteenth century houses
in Lexington Street, still under threat.*
3.   *1732 houses in Broadwick Street,
from Lexington Street. Numerous
attempts at destruction, involving either
gutting or total demolition, have so far
been refused permission.*
4.   *Early eighteenth century houses in
Great Pulteney Street, to be restored
as luxury flats.*
5.   *Brewer Street, block of early
nineteenth century houses to be replaced
by a new office building.*

rehabilitated old house being let at astronomical rents is as useless to Soho as if it were demolished. The only way to save Soho is to return it to its former equilibrium. Only when the speculative element is taken out of land values will they fall enough to let the community of Soho breathe again.

To wrest Soho from the grasp of the speculator demands tough and positive action which is beyond the powers of the Council. Meanwhile the emptying of Soho speeds up. The population is now 2,500. Fourteen per cent of the food shops closed in one year and Berwick Street market is in danger because the disappearing population makes the profit margin dangerously narrow. Soho now contains 300,000 square feet of offices, 170,000 square feet of residential accommodation and 150,000 square feet of empty space.

Westminster, true to form, is planning to make this situation worse rather than better by demolishing the Archer Street dwellings as slums. Two hundred more people will disappear from Soho and their homes will be replaced with flash west-end shops and flats.

Specific threats to Soho accurately reflect the present general threat.

The parish church of St Anne was bombed in the war and consequently demolished by the Church Commissioners. It is now used as a car park. In a deal with the Commissioners, National Car Parks is to dig out the vault, remove the bodies, and construct tier upon tier of parking ramps. For this privilege, NCP will pay the Commissioners about £1½ million. Above the car park the Commissioners will build offices, flats, a clinic and a chapel. All that is now left of the church is Cockerell's peculiar tower which NCP's ramps will undermine at some risk.

The Sutton Settled Estate formed a subsidiary company to develop its property in Brewer Street and Great Pulteney Street. The sixty small firms have been displaced. Permission had been given for the demolition of the early nineteenth century houses in Brewer Street and the partial gutting of the early eighteenth century houses in Great Pulteney Street. All were to be offices and luxury flats. Unfortunately

for the developers, Bruton Investments, a snag has arisen: they have gone bankrupt. So the whole block stands empty and boarded up, awaiting a High Court action.

Also standing boarded up are the early nineteenth century blocks of houses between Marshall Street, Carnaby Street and Foubert's Place. Peachy Estates wanted to demolish them all, but has not obtained Listed Building Consent. Now it has commissioned consultants to try and find ways in which the buildings can be rehabilitated and still make a profit.

6. *7 Poland Street, built in the early eighteenth century, to be demolished.*
7. *Gerrard Street, owned by Stock Conversion Development Company, derelict. Plans for it have included replacement by overhead walkways.*
8. *Early nineteenth century block bordering Carnaby Street, also the subject of numerous unsuccessful applications for permission to destroy.*

138

1

East London is quickly coming to represent London's great lost opportunity. It was devastated in the war and was notorious for its slums so, without a second thought, the decision was taken to 'reconstruct' if after the war. East London became the guinea pig for all the latest planning theories.

The idea was to redevelop comprehensively and by so doing create self-sufficient neighbourhood units. With great vigour, bomb sites were levelled, slums demolished and massive areas designated for slum clearance. By 1960

more of East London was derelict than was devastated during the war. The threat of comprehensive development caused whole areas to stand and rot, and it became obvious that what was being cleared away was not bomb damage and slums, but the very character and history of East London. And because so much of the area was in Council ownership—about 80%—demolition was easy.

Now CDAs declared in the 1960s are still being cleared and, despite mounting public opposition, the Council and the GLC still seem determined not to rest

London~East End

until most of the old, destructive 're-construction' plans have become reality.

The history of East London has worked against it. It has always been London's workshop. When England's empire expanded it was the area east of the City that got the capital's docks and all the trades that went with them. It was the docks that caused East London to grow rapidly so that by the mid eighteenth century the old riverside villages had expanded and linked together to form a linear riverside town that was virtually independent of the rest of London.

This maritime town expanded inland during the later eighteenth century and more old village centres like Stepney and Poplar were absorbed into the sprawling town of East London. This expansion was quickened when the East India Company laid out the Commercial Road in 1800 to connect its docks in the east with the City. Suddenly green fields became accessible for development. At the same time East London's major enclosed docks were being dug out of the marshy river bank. During the early nineteenth century East London continued to be a mixture of the classes—sailors, traders, merchants and factory owners. But its character as the workshop of London became firmly fixed. As the century moved on there was a class polarisation so that by the early twentieth century the rest of London was able to view its eastern portion as a dark and menacing region filled with slum-dwellers and sweatshops. The Victorians tried to improve East London by cutting roads through the slums to 'let in the air'. 100 years later, it was this mentality that underlay the comprehensive development thinking of the 1950s. And it is this mentality that continues to destroy East London now.

Ironically, while vast areas continue to be levelled, East London's greatest opportunity is frozen. The 8½ miles of East London's obsolete dockland, including hundreds of acres of docks, remain in a planners' limbo. The 1973 GLC/DOE Dockland Study has been rejected and now a Joint Develop-

1.   Not much of St Katharine's Dock has survived Taylor Woodrow's redevelopment and a serious fire. 'C' Warehouse, designed by Philip Hardwick, stands empty. Taylor Woodrow has applied for Listed Building Consent to demolish it for 135,000 square feet of offices.
2.   The Tilbury Warehouse, off Commercial Road. Railway warehousing on a gigantic scale, built c. 1885. Current planning proposals treat it as a vacant site.
3.   Listed late-Victorian school. With an adjacent 1740 house in Spital Square, the subject of a current proposal for redevelopment as offices.
4.   This row of five 1804 warehouses in London Docks was involved in applications to demolish in connection with the proposed massive PLA/Sterling Guarantee Trust commercial development. The scheme for the 110-acre site includes 1,000,000 square feet of offices.
5.   Another stack of London Dock warehouses, built in 1811, a beautiful piece of functional architecture. They stand little chance of surviving.
6.   The Wapping Basin of London Dock, when in the process of being filled in. This action was later found to be illegal as the PLA had not applied for planning permission.

ment Committee made up of the GLC, the DOE and the five dockland boroughs is discussing what could be done. But already private developers have grabbed the initiative. Taylor Woodrow got in early and persuaded the GLC to lease it the St Katharine Dock in 1969. It is attempting to build a bit of the City in East London. A huge hotel has already gone up and Taylor Woodrow now want permission to build 776,000 square feet of offices. In the adjacent London Dock, the Port of London Authority and Sterling Guarantee Trust development consortium has put in an application to build 1,000,000 square feet of offices.

So, while much of historic East London is being demolished by the authorities to create opportunities, the same authorities are letting the real opportunity slip from their grip.

7. *Early eighteenth century houses in Redmans Row, down for slum clearance, possibly to be reprieved, but rapidly deteriorating.*
8. *Early nineteenth century chapel in the Tredegar Estate in Bow. While most of the Estate is being rehabilitated, the chapel stands derelict.*
9. *Christ Church, Spitalfields, is still semi-derelict, and the money has not yet been raised for its restoration. Early nineteenth century Brushfield Street, in the foreground, is to be demolished for the expansion of Spitalfields Market.*
10. *Draper's Almshouses in Priscilla Road, Bow, owned by the GLC and derelict for twelve years.*
11. *Early eighteenth century Raine Street School in Wapping, derelict and owned by the GLC.*
12. *Wilkes Street, Spitalfields. A fine 1723 terrace, gradually rotting while the authorities decide how to save it.*
13. *Wapping riverside from Rotherhithe. Six years after the closure of the docks a whole aspect of nineteenth-century commercial London life has vanished, leaving scarcely a trace. The warehouses have gone, to be replaced by a massive hotel and future luxury riverside flats.*
14. *Charringtons have plans to redevelop the site of the Anchor Brewery in Mile*

144

End Road. A fine large group of nineteenth-century industrial buildings will
be lost, and the scheme threatens the
uniquely secluded Bellevue Place and this
1730 terrace which faces on the Mile
End Road.

15. Mount Terrace, Whitechapel. The
London Hospital will demolish these
Listed buildings as part of their expan-
sion programme.

16, 17. The London Hospital was built
in 1751, and extended at various periods.
The younger Charles Barry's Alexandra
Wing, foreground, 17, has just been
demolished and only fragments of the
early nineteenth-century planned estate
behind the Hospital will remain, 16.

18. Bromley Street. One of the last of
East London's characteristic early
nineteenth century two-storey terraces.
Owned by the GLC, it is boarded up awaiting its probable fate.

17

18

Manchester

Manchester's main street, Piccadilly, runs the gauntlet of two great holes in the ground. The hole on the east side will be filled by Manchester Corporation's and Town and City Properties' Arndale Centre. This will consist of five large stores, 200 shops, a market hall, a bus station, a car park for 2,000 cars, and 200,000 square feet of offices. This scheme will link up with the other large hole on the west side of the street which is known as the Market Cross Development. These two commercial centres will be linked by the predictable overhead walkways. In Market Street, to the north of Piccadilly, the Corporation has declared another large Comprehensive Development Area which is being developed by Central and District Properties, to provide 72,000 square feet of commercial space, 282,000 square feet of offices, and 710 car parking spaces—all on the site of the now obliterated Shambles. This is merely phase one: a second phase is to follow on an adjacent site. Developments of this scale and size are virtually obliterating the history of the city.

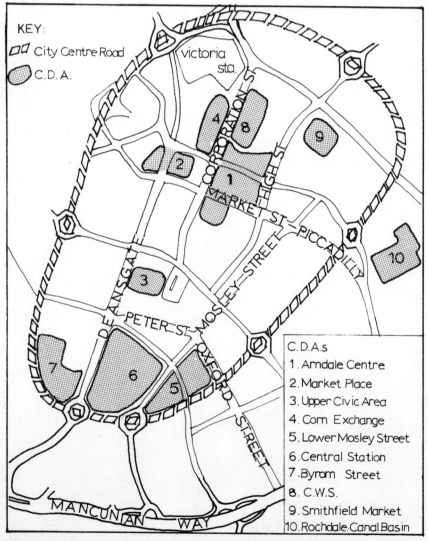

KEY:
▢▢ City Centre Road
◯ C.D.A.

C.D.A.s
1. Arndale Centre
2. Market Place
3. Upper Civic Area
4. Corn Exchange
5. Lower Mosley Street
6. Central Station
7. Byrom Street
8. C.W.S.
9. Smithfield Market
10. Rochdale Canal Basin

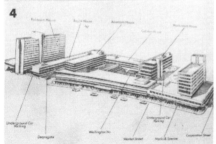

From its Georgian and medieval centre Manchester grew at great speed during the Industrial Revolution into a true Victorian city. Late-Victorian commercial and public buildings standing on a Victorian street pattern gave Manchester a scale based on the warehouse and not, as in London, on domestic buildings. It is this unique nineteenth-century quality that modern development has done its best to destroy in the massive redevelopment areas that totally ignore the nature of the city. The area around the Old Corn Exchange is now a mass of rapidly emptying Victorian commercial buildings that are doomed to be demolished. The Listed Corn Exchange itself is to be demolished, and the Corporation is making clearance easier for the developers by making use of its compulsory powers. Albert Square, the setting for Waterhouse's Town Hall, one of the great Victorian Gothic monuments of the north of England, is to be redeveloped through to Deansgate by the Heron Group to include a twelve-storey tower block set back from Deansgate.

The Listed Central Railway Station, closed by British Rail in 1965, forms the centre of a 23-acre CDA. English and Continental Properties has acquired it from British Rail and at present the

1. *Where the Smithfield market stood. The site is to become a car park.*
2. *The new-look Piccadilly.*
3. *High Street, Manchester: a hole belonging to Town and City Properties.*
4, 5. *The Market Place CDA. This development when completed will incorporate the sad relics of the Shambles.*
6. *The shed of the Central Station forms the centre of a 23-acre CDA. Now used as a car park, it may survive as a display centre, but its future is not yet secure.*
7. *The Listed Corn Exchange, due to be demolished as part of the Corn Exchange CDA.*
8. *A warehouse within the Central Station CDA which will not survive.*
9. *Late eighteenth century houses in the Smithfield area, derelict since the market moved.*

old platforms are leased to National Car Parks. There is hope that it may survive as an exhibition centre, but its future cannot yet be seen as assured. The adjoining huge brick railway warehouses are not protected. The City envisages 1,000,000 square feet of offices being built on the site, five acres of which will go for the proposed City Centre Road. Victoria Station, which incorporates a block of Stephenson's early station, is soon to be partly redeveloped. Manchester's food markets have been moved from the central area at Smithfield to the city's boundary. The City Corporation may still redevelop their sites. This would involve the demolition of the few remaining eighteenth-century terraces and shops in the city, as well as of the large Victorian Market Buildings. The Corporation has also applied for consent to demolish the 1870 Fish Market. Some of these large covered spaces could certainly have been given new uses in any redevelopment. The best Art Nouveau building in Manchester, 18-20 Oxford Street, is now part of a 4-acre CDA and it is likely to be demolished. India House in Whitworth Street, a magnificant Edwardian office block, should be Listed; its owner is trying to demolish it. Even the City is anxious to keep this building. In York Street a remarkably rich Edwardian Baroque bank built in 1902 and full of marble columns and lofty ceilings, is to be demolished. Immediately opposite a new concrete bank is being erected, its quality forcing one to ask why such good buildings are being demolished for such mediocre replacements.

10. *Interior of the 1870 Fish Market. The Corporation's plans for the site are uncertain but it is likely to be demolished.*
11. *India House in Whitworth Street. It may still be demolished.*
12. *Permission has been given for the demolition of this fine Edwardian Baroque bank in York Street.*
13. *Detail of a panel on the Fish Market.*
14. *Exterior of the Fish Market and a row of doomed nineteenth-century shops.*

13

OPENED : 14 : FEB : 1873 : BOOTH : MAYOR

14

Salisbury

ALL ENQUIRIES CONCERNING
OFFICE DEVELOPMENT
ON THIS SITE
OSMOND, TRICKS
AND SON
T.&.R QUEEN SQUARE BRISTOL. BS1 4JL

4

Constable's famous view of Salisbury Cathedral over the placid water meadows remains remarkably intact, and the visitor's first impression is that all is well. But signs that the commercial acquisitiveness of the chain stores is compromising the real historic character of the town quickly become noticeable.

Right in the centre Hammerson's Old George Mall development has succeeded in hiding away a large area of new shoping space behind the existing frontages—except on the south side, where the blank, featureless sterility of the access area and three-storey car park stretches down the length of New Street in bizarre contrast to the classic 'old world' street that remains facing it. (The car park also has an irredeemably crushing effect on the first-class Georgian house at No. 4 New Street, which survives next to it, and its harsh horizontal lines appear shouldering up against ancient buildings through a breach in the street line round the corner in Catherine Street.) But the authenticity of the buildings that have been left is diminished by the filling in of the area they once backed on to, while nonsense has been made of the structure of the timber-framed Old George itself, which has lost its ground floor to the main entrance of the Mall. Equally serious for the city is the way in which the development attracts a high volume of traffic right into the centre, the car parks and the concrete environment being the most obvious physical reminder of it.

Elsewhere a number of important buildings are being subjected to the same combination of conservation and castration, and others are being simply demolished in numbers that are small but all the more significant in a city of such extraordinary completeness and richness. The Cross Keys Chequer site on the market place is one of the principal victims. Over the past ten years there has been a series of proposals for a block of buildings on the west side of the Cross Keys Chequer, along Queen Street. All the buildings are Listed. The earliest surviving parts of this complex are No. 14 and the former Plume of Feathers Inn surrounding a courtyard. No. 14 still retains a jettied

front onto the street and its roof structure is intact. A late fourteenth century timber-framed building discovered inside the courtyard may still be demolished and the developer wants to roof in the courtyard itself with a plastic covering. Nos. 18 and 19 had a fine eighteenth-century staircase and elegant plasterwork on the drawing room ceiling. This plasterwork has been destroyed; the staircase may be put back. The latest proposals for the site take the form of most radical 'rehabilitation'. An enormous open-plan office at first floor level will run from the jettied building to the corner of Winchester Street. At night when all the fluorescent tubes are burning bright, any illusion that this is an historic building will be lost. No. 14 can hardly remain standing as a timber-framed building—if these plans are followed through it will simply be another facsimile.

Close to the Cross Keys site Nos. 19 and 21 Winchester Street, Listed Grade II*, a sixteenth-century building refaced about 1800, with a seventeenth-century rear wing, is now definitely at risk. It has been empty for five years, deteriorating rapidly, and is now on offer for office redevelopment. No. 88 Milford Street, a sixteenth-century timber-framed house, was moved to this site in the nineteenth century. Listed Grade II*, it was demolished for the new Churchill Way road with the intention that it should be re-erected by the Council. In fact it still lies in a Council store and there is no sign yet of its re-erection.

Pressures on the town from through traffic have eased since the completion of the eastern arm of Churchill Way, but this road does come far too near the centre of the city, slicing communities in half and carving up gardens. The road has involved the loss of No. 88 Milford Street and corresponding buildings at the end of St Ann Street and Winchester Street. Far more ludicrously damaging is the expensive elevated feeder road which sails over the small-scale streets, flying into nowhere. It may one day lead into a multi-storey car park that has yet to be built in Brown Street; a more hopeful chance is that it may be demolished.

1. Salisbury's folly. Will this road ever reach the multi-storey car park which it was meant to lead to?
2. The cleared site behind the Queen Street facades in the Cross Keys Chequer.
3. 19 and 21 Winchester Street, medieval with an eighteenth-century front, empty for years and now on offer for office development.
4. Facadism at work in the Cross Keys Chequer. Behind the retained fronts there will be an air-conditioned shopping centre with a Safeway supermarket, twenty-two shop units and open-plan offices running the entire length of the building.
5. Partial conservation in New Street. One side is more or less untouched but has to look at the endless car park that has consumed almost the whole of the opposite side.
6. 19 and 21 Winchester Street in relation to surrounding buildings.

Truro

In the eighteenth century Truro grew from a small market town into the centre of fashionable Cornish society. Large town houses were built in Princes Street and Lemon Street. The prosperity generated by the growth of Cornish industry in the late eighteenth century, especially tin mining, is reflected in the city's fabric. In 1880 the Cathedral began to rise above a town extended by the building of commercial and manufacturing buildings, workers' cottages and docks.

In 1965 the city built a relief road that finally severed the heart of the town

from its river. For some reason the Council wants to join the all-embracing arms of the relief road by cutting a new road through Lemon Street, the finest street in Truro. This proposed radial route will not only destroy houses in Lemon Street but will also turn Fairmantle Street into a fast main road and demolish one side of Charles Street.

Related to these road proposals are four large multi-storey car parks. Two have already been built, one of them sited behind Lemon Street, where the streets are too narrow for the traffic. One of those proposed will ruin forever,

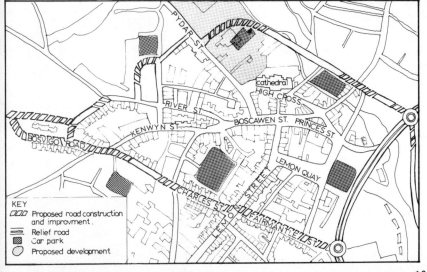

the old town green and the Lemon Street Quay. Both of these spaces are vital to Truro in terms of history and amenity. The green, which is owned publicly, is at present kept by the Council as a piece of tarmac with trees poking through. The Quay, which was bridged over in the 1930s, retains its granite dock walls and steps beneath its concrete lid. The other site for a car park lies immediately beside the east end of the Cathedral. But the new Council upset a deal made by the old for its development, and the future of the site is now uncertain.

A car park that did get built stands just to the north of the Cathedral and is only a part of the huge High Cross shopping and office development for the Hearts of Oak property investment fund.

Hearts of Oak have been acquiring land in the town centre for more than fifteen years and they now own so much that the new County Council has to negotiate with the company to buy land for new Crown Courts, a library and Council offices. In view of the extent of their land holdings in the city it is almost certain that another large-scale development on Lemon Quay is on the cards—a development that the city does not need.

1. *The Cathedral from Bosvigo Road area. A new road will demolish some of these small terraces and blight those that remain.*
2. *Lemon Street, a classic English eighteenth-century street, has survived almost intact until now. The two houses in the left foreground are to be demolished by their owners, and a central section of the street faces the threat of demolition for road widening.*
3. *A new view of the Cathedral from the east. The large vacant site will accommodate a multi-storey car park and a supermarket.*
4. *Lemon Quay with the covered-over dock in the foreground and the old Green on the left. The City plans to build a permanent car park on both of these. The Hearts of Oak Building Society are acquiring the buildings behind for a future large-scale development.*
5. *Lemon Street. This corner and the one opposite are threatened by road widening.*
6. *The new car park, obscuring views of the Cathedral from the river.*

162

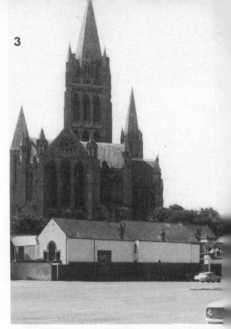

3

4

5

Wisbech

2

The character of Wisbech as a perfect Georgian market town and Fenland port has recently been evoked for us by the publication of Samuel Smith's wonderful Victorian photographs. Only the obviously good parts of Wisbech now remain in reasonable repair; they are the two streets that border the River Nene—North Brink and South Brink. The town still serves the surrounding agricultural community as a trading centre, and its centre is now dominated by the standard frontages of the chain stores, especially in the New Market Place. The Old Market Place now has a derelict air—at its centre is a public lavatory surrounded by a tarmac car park. This is the centre of the town's declining area.

On the north side there is a perfect small early Georgian terrace house

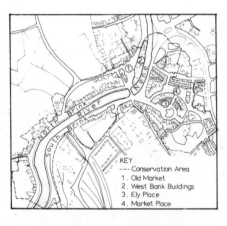

KEY:
--- Conservation Area
1. Old Market
2. West Bank Buildings
3. Ely Place
4. Market Place

(dated 1723) which is being left quietly to slip into decay; a Victorian sale room and a white-painted eighteenth-century building both stand empty. The most crucial, and most threatened, building on the Old Market is No. 8/9. A broad and tall pedimented mid-eighteenth-century house, it has been allowed to stand empty for years.

Behind No. 8/9 are the magnificent early nineteenth century warehouses that stand on the River Nene and are known as the West Bank Buildings.

Wisbech once had many such warehouses when it was a prosperous inland port. In the nineteenth century, even sea-going ships were able to navigate the Nene as far as Wisbech and the Georgian houses on the North Brink were screened by the masts and ropes of ships moored many-deep in the river. Now, this group on the west bank is all that survives. They are empty and rotting. A report has been published by the architects Fielden and Mawson and Ove Arup & Partners to show how these warehouses could be saved and what use they could be converted to. But, as so often, money is not forthcoming and the warehouses continue to slip slowly into the Nene.

North from the Old Market Place the town dissolves into a vacuous spread of new roads and indifferent new buildings. A massively out-of-scale road that should have been built well away from Wisbech now cuts through the edges of the town—an amazingly de-- structive feat for a small town that is totally surrounded by flat land. This dreary new road has collected around

itself several new buildings that presumably represent the town's efforts to be up-to-date. Right alongside the busy new main road is the new hospital, perhaps the ugliest new hospital in the country, a collection of random sheds grouped around a huge chimney, and certainly among the most oddly sited.

There is no lack of confidence in Wisbech when it comes to housing: mediocre housing estates have spread with great speed. Council housing is destined to surround Mounpesson House, a large and distinguished house, isolated outside the Conservation Areas, now empty and surrounded by wrecked cars and shops selling second-hand motor accessories. The Baptist Cemetery, now romantically overgrown, is likely to vanish under a municipal 'improvement' plan to turn it into a public garden.

1.   *The West Bank Buildings in 1974, the warehouses derelict and in danger. Expensive plans exist for the repair of some of them, but they are only plans.*
2.   *The West Bank Buildings as they were in the town's maritime prime in the mid nineteenth century*
3.   *Doorcase of Mounpesson House.*
4.   *The North Brink—the most historic part of Wisbech presents a well-polished face to the world.*
5.   *Mounpesson House. The elegance of the eighteenth century at sea in a derelict area zoned for council housing.*
6.   *8/9 Old Market Place has been neglected to the point where it is now in danger of collapse.*

Ashford

'Ashford is changing rapidly and throughout the town old buildings are disappearing to make way for new.' 'Ashford has for a long time been overshadowed by other towns in the area. It is now beginning to come into its own.' 'Bulldozers, pneumatic drills, mechanical diggers and giant cranes are becoming a familiar sight in the town. The noise of progress can be depressing for residents. But it has to be endured as the town builds itself into a better place.'

'Modern office blocks bear witness to large-scale investment in the town. One such is the Charter Consolidated building.' 'Small office blocks are also

pushing skywards around the town.' 'A new shopping precinct to rival that of any new town is starting to take shape in Hempsted Street.'

'Driving in from the A20, up from Folkestone, the motorist can sense things are on the move at Ashford. The only trouble is... the road network into the town leaves much to be desired.' 'The new ring road and other road plans will ease the problem.'

'In building for the future care is being taken to preserve the best of the old to

1. *Ashford.*
2. *'Part of old Ashford gives way to the new as construction goes ahead on the Hempstead Street shopping precinct.'*
3. *'This is the partly completed Charter Consolidated building which towers over a street of buildings of quite a different generation.'*

achieve an equilibrium in the town of which its inhabitants will feel justifiably proud.' 'A walk behind the chain stores and supermarkets reveals a careful preservation of Ashford's heritage. Shopkeepers' signs—"established 1700"—and buildings behind the Old Cottage in North Street—itself dating back to 1370—remind us of our history. Still at the centre, St Mary's Parish Church, with 500 years of history, serves a changing community.'

'If the visitor on foot is just here for the sights then Ashford has its historical tank to offer, its parks and a walk by the river.'

(Text, pictures and captions for this chapter are taken from a supplement to the *Kentish Express* dated April 1974. The arrangement of the quoted excerpts is not the same as in the original.)

4. *'The route of the new ring road.'*
5. *'The tank—one of Ashford's best known landmarks. A relic of the past preserved amid the new.'*

And....

1. Baldock. *This fine early eighteenth century house, once part of a brewery, is being allowed to decay. Although it forms a vital part of an outstanding street, the local authority does nothing effective to make the owner arrest the rapid decay.*

2, 3. Canterbury. *Seventeenth-century houses in North Lane threatened by Council road improvement plans, 2. Early nineteenth century houses in the green setting of the Dane John, 3. The Council has plans for demolition.*

4. Cockermouth. *This impressively complete eighteenth-century market town on a medieval street pattern is about to lose a central part of its market place. The Chamber of Commerce wants to redevelop 9-25 Market Street. All are Listed.*

5. Devizes. *Timber-framed house to be demolished for road widening.*

6. Didcot. *Seventeenth-century farm-house within the shadow of the power*

station, *stands derelict.*

7. Edenbridge. *These vernacular early nineteenth century timber framed cottages just off the High Street were to have been demolished for a hotel, and remain empty.*

8. Exeter. *St Edmund's Church, partially demolished without planning permission.*

174

9, 10. Halifax. *The Square Congregational Church,* **9,** *was built in 1855 by
Joseph James. The tower, derived from
Pugin's church at Cheadle, dominates
the city and is especially striking as
seen from the classical colonnades of
the Peice Market. Demolition proceeds.
Next to the Congregational Church is
an earlier Congregational Chapel,* **10.**
*It was built in 1772 and is now obsolete
and vandalised.*

11, 12, 13. Huntingdon. *Seventeenth-
century house in the High Street up for
redevelopment,* **11.** *Another,* **12,** *by the
church awaits a similar fate. A large
mill beside the medieval bridge,* **13,** *has
been blown up twice but refuses to fall
down. It is not Listed, so the owner will
try again.*

14. Lewes. *The Council compulsorily
purchased many of the town's smaller
eighteenth-century buildings for road
works. The road has been abandoned,
but the empty buildings continue to rot.*

175

15. London, Bloomsbury. *Woburn Square, built in 1830. The University is still determined to demolish.*
16. London, Brentford. *Derelict early nineteenth century pair on the edge of the Grand Union Canal.*
17. London, Bromley. *Late seventeenth century house in the High Street, empty and open to vandals.*

18. London, Camberwell. *Camberwell New Road was laid out and built along in the 1820s. It survives as a uniquely complete example of early nineteenth century London ribbon development consisting of villas and terraces. A quarter of a mile of it is to be demolished by the GLC for roads and slum clearance.*

19. London, Clerkenwell. *St Luke's, Old Street, designed in the 1730s by Nicholas Hawksmoor, was blasted in the war and 'made safe'—the roof and interior taken down—by the Church Commissioners in 1965. Now only the extraordinary tower and shell survive. The Commissioners wanted to demolish it but may now have relented.*

20. London, Euston. *The fight to save the community around North Gower Street from massive commercial redevelopment by Stock Conversion continues. These early nineteenth century houses, all owned by the developers, still rot.*

21. London, Fitzroy Square Area. *Early nineteenth century Warren Street, decayed and now being demolished.*

22. London, Fulham. *The pottery, which dates from the sixteenth century, is to be demolished for an office development.*
23. London, Goode Street Area. *Goode Place, built in the late eighteenth century, is blighted because of the long-standing plan of the adjacent Middlesex Hospital to expand onto the site.*
24. London, Hackney. *The Paragon, an early nineteenth century parade of unique design, is owned by the Council, which wants to demolish it.*
25. London, Hammersmith. *London Transport is to redevelop the Hammersmith Station site, demolishing the present bus garage which was converted from Thomas Archer's eighteenth century manor house, Bradmore House.*
26. London, Hyde Park Corner. *Wilkins' early nineteenth century St George's Hospital will be obsolete in 1980.*
27, 28. London, Islington. *The Royal Agricultural Hall, built in 1860, 27, was Listed after being bought by a developer, who has now applied to demolish it. The Angel pub, built in 1901, 28, a magnificent terracotta monument at the junction of City Road, Pentonville Road and Upper Street, is to be demolished for road widening.*

29. London, St Paul's Cray. *Late seventeenth century row, a remarkable combination of vernacular and early classical, perfectly alive and well but in the path of a road widening scheme.*

30. London, Southwark. *St Saviour's Dock, formerly the Jacob's Island of Oliver Twist, is an inlet from the Thames lined with nineteenth-century warehouses. Most are obsolete and all are due for demolition. Shad Thames, a winding, narrow medieval street on Southwark's riverside, is similarly lined with high Victorian warehouses, all to be demolished as part of the Hay's Wharf redevelopment and replaced with offices designed by Richard Seifert.*

31. London, Stepney. *Parfett Street, a rare early nineteenth century street of miniature three-storey houses, unlisted. Tower Hamlets Council has initiated slum clearance procedures.*

32. London, Stoke Newington. *Two superb large early eighteenth century houses in the High Street stand derelict. One is owned by the DOE, which originally wanted to demolish it but has now relented. The other has been empty for ten years.*

33. London, Temple. *Early nineteenth century lodge in Strand Lane standing*

in the way of the expansion of King's College, London, to be demolished.

34. London, Tottenham. *Dial House in the High Street, 1697, derelict.*

35, 36. London, Trafalgar Square. *Two development companies propose to re-develop the entire south east corner of the Square. Land Securities wants to replace the 1876 Grand Buildings, 35, with the same amount of offices at rents roughly six times as high. The United Kingdom Provident Institution plans to replace the block of buildings between Northumberland Avenue and Whitehall, 36, with new offices and shops.*

37. London, Vauxhall. *Brunswick House, formerly a riverside mansion, now marooned by roads and cold storage depots, in the ownership of British Rail. It is unlikely to last long under these conditions.*

38, 39. London, Victoria. *60 Buckingham Gate. Hills Hygienic Bakery was built in 1876 to the designs of T. Verity, 38. Despite its being Listed, the GLC has given Sterling Land permission to de-molish. One of the key reasons for this decision was Westminster's request to have the building down so that it could implement a 1952 road-widening scheme. Wellington House, 39. Land Securities*

has been given permission by Westminster City Council to demolish this fine 1906 Baroque building and build expensive offices on the site.

40. London, Wanstead. *Fine early eighteenth century houses let as flats, in a neglected condition and under threat.*

41. London, Westminster. *Parliament Street, a mixture of eighteenth-century*

domestic and Victorian commercial buildings, to be demolished for the new Parliament building.

42, 43. Maidstone. *Much has been destroyed in Maidstone since the war, and much of what remains now stands threatened. Early nineteenth century Holy Trinity, 42, is derelict and due to be demolished. Lower Stone Street, 43, a fine collection of sixteenth-, seven-*

42

43

teenth-, and eighteenth-century buildings
stands derelict and decayed. On the
town's past record of demolition it is
likely many of these will go.
44, 45. Margate. *More than half the
buildings in the core of the town stand
derelict and under threat of demolition.
The victims range from a group of early
nineteenth century terraces,* 44, *to
individual early eighteenth century*

houses, 45.
46. Penzance. *These houses will be
lost when the town builds its ring road.*
47. Preston. *Around Preston's
Georgian Winckley Square a network of
early nineteenth century streets
survives. The Council is planning
massive clearances.*
48. Royston. *A street of late medieval*

44

48

45

49

46

50

47

houses stands boarded up, rotting and awaiting its fate.

49. St Ives, Cornwall. *This late eighteenth century granite house in the Stennack is due for demolition to make way for a relief road. In order to widen the Stennack, the Council has already at great expense covered over a stream parallel to the road.*

50. St Ives, Huntingdon. *Seventeenth-century houses each side of the approach to the medieval bridge stand derelict. An application has been made for the demolition of two Listed buildings in the Broadway.*

51. Scarborough. *King Street, in a Conservation Area and containing Listed buildings, will be dissected by a new road if the North Riding County Council's plans are carried out.*

52. Towednack. *This small chapel is up for sale for the second time in two years, damaged and unrepaired following winter storms. It is typical of the multitude of Cornish chapels, many now disused and with a very uncertain future.*

53, 54. Ware. *The group of seventeenth- and eighteenth-century buildings in Star Street, 53, will go if Hertfordshire County Council is successful at a DOE public inquiry and is given permission to build its inner relief road. After smashing through these houses, the road loops behind Ware, cutting through the seventeenth-century Crib Street, 54, and joins the top of Baldock Street.*

55. Wellingborough. *The town's fine tithe barn stands isolated and decaying.*

Conclusion

This is a depressing book. It has looked at thirty British towns and found the forces of 'redevelopment' successfully ruining them all. Its tone is strident because the situation is, in many places, so bad that only a complete change of attitude can save our cities.

Towns are centres of sociability, places where the mind is exercised by frequent contact with other minds and where the eyes are enlivened by a townscape that encapsulates in buildings the history of our society. But what do we see in these sociable centres today? Most of the towns that have acquired new centres in the postwar years have lost their old hearts and received in return transplants of vacuity.

We have tried to show simply that we care deeply for the past, and particularly for the old buildings that are the past, and we are gravely concerned that so much of our heritage is in great danger. It may surprise many readers that things are so bad. Surely the laws are there to protect the environment. Surely the conservation societies and the pressure groups are stronger than they have ever been. And people are becoming more aware—they visit the country houses, accept and enjoy programmes about their heritage on the television, and are taking a very much larger part in the planning of their own areas. But the man in the street is as nothing alongside the thrusting power of corporate commercial greed. There is no doubt that it is the pressure to use the city simply as a base for private profit-making that has created the havoc in our towns. Conservation groups working voluntarily in their members' spare time have little chance of making a serious impact. The developers, on the other hand, are full-time, highly paid and with large qualified staffs. And the general public, although better informed and 'knowing what it likes', is nonetheless intimidated by the professionals and left feeling completely powerless when it comes up against the steep bastions of bureaucracy.

Another powerful influence on the shape of Britain's towns has been the activities of the architectural and planning professions. The grisly results of their trade are there, in almost all our towns, lasting memorials to an age of little taste and less sensitivity. Since the early 1950s architects trained in the disciplines and dogmas of an alien 'Modern Movement' have imposed an architecture on small towns and historic city centres that simply does not fit. The public has realised for a long time that there is something wrong with modern architecture. It is more difficult for a trained professional to re-think his old doctrines and admit that he has littered our cities with far too many shoddy and irrational structures. Of course, there are a few exceptions to this generalisation, but these are often confined to the remote world of the universities or the rich private client, and unfortunately good modern architecture has had little effect on the everyday market place. Even housing schemes have been built to fit in with curious dogmas—the propaganda for the tower block is only just being seriously and effectively questioned. There are too many windswept plazas, too many elephantine shopping centres, and there is too much drawing board planning that bears little relation to the existing city.

The massive, and necessary, building and reconstruction boom that followed the Second World War is now at an end. Fortunes have been made and lost and cities have been wrecked and despoiled. Only the sudden rise in the price of oil and the slump in the world's stock markets has forced a questioning of our blind faith in 'growth'.

What effect does the energy crisis and the economic state of the West have on the state of our towns? Essentially the end of cheap fuel means a limitation on production, movement and growth. This shortage of energy need not provoke an extreme reaction of the 'back to nature' variety, but it must end the headlong rush for technological expansion. In our cities it could mean an end to cancerous and undifferentiated growth, and a return to a steadier, more natural process of change and development. We may hope that in architecture there will be a greater realisation of the value of old buildings, and a policy of rehabilitation rather than demolition whenever it is feasible. There could be a qualitative improvement in building—better rather than more.

Perhaps it is too easy to blame the architect and the developer for everything. Could these great changes have happened if the public had had a different attitude to their cities? The Victorian growth of towns initiated the great debate about the city and society. Many Victorian writers saw their time as an 'age of great cities'—the city was as much a matter for pride as it was a matter for humanitarian concern. Sudden growth and redevelopment is not entirely new: what has changed is man's vision of the city. A planner's utopia today no longer matches the dreams of the man in the street. Only now are planning officials beginning to realise that large-scale comprehensive clearance is wrong. In an area like Covent Garden in London, it has taken almost five years of active work by the community to convince the planners that the area should not be comprehensively developed. Only through public awareness was this centre of London saved from a monolithic, concrete redevelopment, surrounded by a ring of new wide roads. Other cities have had less luck.

Somewhere beneath all the plans and blueprints, and the traffic engineer's diagrams, lie the old buildings that are the past of our cities. Their fate has until relatively recently been secondary to the process of rebuilding. Thousands have been cynically destroyed, not that they were beyond repair or dangerous, but simply because they stood in the way of the developer's vision of the new city, or of his new bank balance. Old buildings mean a great deal more than their fabric. As their number decreases daily, those who care for the past simply have to shout more loudly to save what they can. The law is gradually being strengthened to protect historic buildings, but what is not changing is the attitude of planning officials to the past. Preservationists run the risk of appearing paranoid but it has so often been necessary to be shrill before anything is changed. The city of Bath is a perfect example—opposition to the City Corporation's development plans had to reach screaming pitch before anything was done. If a national furore is necessary to save somewhere as obviously historic and beautiful as Bath, think how difficult it is likely to be to save the minor glories of some other less famous towns.

Our concern is not a new one. It is worth recalling the feelings of William Morris writing about Oxford in 1853, before he had founded the Society for the Protection of Ancient Buildings. 'Oxford in those days still kept a great deal of its earlier loveliness: and the memory of its grey streets as they then were has been an abiding influence and pleasure in my life—and would be greater still if I could only forget what they are now, a matter of far more importance than the so-called learning of the place could have been to me.... The guardians of this beauty and romance so fertile of education, though professedly engaged in the "higher education" (as the futile system of compromise they follow is nick-named), have ignored it utterly, have made its preservation give way to the pressure of commercial exigencies and are determined apparently to destroy it altogether. There is another pleasure for the world gone down the wind; here, again, the beauty and romance have been uselessly, causelessly, most foolishly thrown away.... It has been sold at a cheap price indeed: muddled away by the greed and incompetence of fools who do not know what life and pleasure mean, who will neither take them themselves nor let others have them.'

Despite his pioneering work in the foundation of the SPAB and the subsequent work of Morris's disciples, Listed buildings are still not safe. One Listed building is still being lost almost every day of the year. This figure is based on the statistics provided by the Department of the Environment. Naturally the percentage of Listed buildings demolished has decreased over the last few years as so many more buildings are being Listed—the present total is around 240,000. Conservation Areas, legislation, pressure groups all help to preserve buildings, but it is a disturbing fact that they continue to disappear. Only increased vigilance and more public education about the values of the past and their lessons for today can help to save the remnants of our heritage.

To lose all sense of the sequences of time in our towns is an irreparable loss. Villages and small towns were built evidence of that benign practicality that drew people into workable communities. The great cities are plainly too large and as the cheap fuel flows away, there will be a realisation of the value of living and working in smaller communities. The shortages of materials will ensure that every building is seen as part of the national stock; an awareness will be forced upon us of the real value of bricks and mortar. The ersatz growth encouraged by inflation will slowly stop and the relationship between growth and improvement will again become apparent. All this will only be possible if the political control of our environment passes into more responsive hands. This is particularly crucial at the local level where, in the recent past, too many members of planning committees have been estate agents and too few have had any knowledge or advice about historic buildings at their disposal. Above all, it is architects and planners who must now realise that mass-produced buildings are no longer a social panacea. Mass-produced environments create a suitable world only for the slaves of the production line. Daily there is ample evidence that this kind of slavery to technology is evil.

There is once again a public feeling for architecture both old and new. It is the professionals that have been caught on the hop. The environmental professions have learned a great deal, in the last thirty years or so, about industrialisation, management techniques, sociology, and building science, but they have not succeeded in producing a new architecture that works and is satisfying to the eye and the intellect. Professionals, like so many artists and writers, have moved off into their own esoteric worlds. Mercifully the slow grinding of the gears of the progress machine has forced them back onto the streets. And it is these streets that this book is all about. These streets bear the imprint of years of human activity—they are the character of our society. The enforced slowing down in economic growth is in fact an opportunity to be seized. It may be the last chance to redeem the streets where we live and work. Britain has suffered enormously in the last thirty years, but the true shape of that suffering is not to be seen in the newspapers or on the television screens. The social history of Britain is written in her towns; open your eyes and learn from the recent past. The lessons are writ large, in concrete. Is it too late to save and enhance the little that remains?

How To Stop It

The atrocities chronicled in this book are taking place despite the existence of laws designed to protect historic buildings and historic areas of towns and cities. But the law provides the main hope of arresting the headlong torrent of destruction until the effects of the energy crisis and the slowdown in economic growth work themselves out in the development process. The law will work, given a real will to conserve on the part of local and national government, and this political will can be successfully instilled by the amenity societies, national and local, and by the cumulative pressure of the voices of concerned individuals, working through amenity societies and directly, by writing letters to officials and elected representatives.

A new element was introduced into the legislation by the Civic Amenities Act 1967. Previously the law had paid attention only to individual buildings (or small groups of buildings) of merit that might be Listed (we have seen the limitations even of this protection, in terms of inadequate staff to catch up with the backlog of Listing, and the rate of destruction of Listed buildings). Now for the first time areas of townscape could receive limited protection by being designated Conservation Areas. The Town and Country Amenities Act 1974 has at last given Conservation Area designation the teeth which it previously lacked, by bringing the demolition of all buildings within Conservation Areas under the same control as Listed buildings. It also enables the DOE to designate Conservation Areas—previously it was the exclusive responsibility of often reluctant local authorities—and it increases the likelihood of something effective being done in the face of that most insidious technique for bringing a valuable old building to its knees—neglect. Before the Act, the only sanction available to back up the issue of a Repairs Notice was compulsory purchase, and local authorities were usually deterred from issuing Notices by the thought of the expense they might be landed with. Now the price the local authority has to pay for a building acquired under these circumstances is no longer affected by the development potential of the site; and, most important, government as well as local authority can now execute repairs, on Listed buildings and on buildings in Conservation Areas, and recover the cost from the owner. This means too that the government can act against local authorities that neglect buildings in their own ownership.

Finally, if the proposals resulting from the Dobry Review of the Development Control System become effective, the principle that the public has a stake in the physical shape of its surroundings will be extended beyond the bounds of designated Conservation Areas to bring under control the demolition of any building.

An outstanding problem still to be dealt with is the unrestrained power of District Surveyors (or their equivalent) over historic buildings. If a District Surveyor thinks any building is in a dangerous condition, he has *carte blanche* to order its destruction. A recent very grave loss of early eighteenth century houses in an intact street, designated an Outstanding Conservation Area—Great Ormond Street in London, next door to the SPAB—resulted from this situation. Listed buildings should surely be dealt with by specially qualified DSs—or there should be an emergency procedure requiring that, before a DS can place a Dangerous Structure Notice on a Listed building, he must call in a 'flying squad' of DOE officials experienced in the sympathetic handling of old buildings, to certify that no alternative remedies to demolition exist.

Churches are not yet properly protected. The churches still remain exempt from planning control—and ineligible for financial assistance; and the arrangements for dealing with redundant churches positively require that they should be demolished if no use can be found for them—except where they are of 'special merit'. Still, too, government departments and 'statutory undertakers' are largely free to do what they like with their buildings.

More legislative opportunity means more voluntary responsibility. Public authorities must be kept up to the intentions expressed in the legislation, and the potential—and the need—for informed comment and advice to supplement the limited resources of expert manpower available to government and council is vastly expanded.

The greatest burden falls on the national amenity societies, already hard pressed by the accelerating rate of applications for consent to demolish Listed buildings. Their grant from the government in recognition of its dependence on them for comments on these applications must be greatly increased from the present tiny £4,000 a year per society. They also need more money if they are to carry out properly the larger task of getting over the message of conservation to architects, planners, local politicians, the media and the public, and fostering local action for conservation. In this they must remain independent of government support, and they do need a greatly expanded membership. *Join one or more of the national societies if you have not done so already.* Their addresses are given below.

Apart from getting more money to fight for conservation on a national scale and to put the expert point of view wherever the need arises up and down the country, the national societies must adopt a new approach to the battle. Their primary role in the past has been in relation to individual buildings, pressing for Listing and opposing applications to demolish Listed buildings—and the division of responsibility between the SPAB, the Georgian Group and the Victorian Society reflects this. Now they must work on a wider front for the designation of Conservation Areas and the defence of all buildings within Conservation Areas that contribute to the collective character of the townscape. Here too they must offer their services to the public authorities and demand that they are given further government support in recompense for providing assistance on which the government depends for the carrying out of its intentions expressed in legislation.

But the opportunity for the national societies to act and act effectively depends in nearly all cases on the information and support they receive from local amenity societies, action groups and individuals. (It is only applications to demolish Listed buildings that have to be notified to the national societies, and for many of these the application does not contain enough information about the building for the society to be able to comment without getting a local report.) The people on the ground know their buildings, know or can find out when threats arise, and are in the best position to influence local authorities to act. If you have been moved by this book and recognise the same destructive processes at work in the area where you live, *you can do something about it directly, now,* by joining and taking an active part in your local society or action group (you can find out about it from the Town Hall). If no local group exists, you can probably affect the situation quite dramatically by forming one. Write to the national societies and ask for the names of members in your area; contact local architects, teachers, social workers and other professionals that are likely to be interested; use the hospitality of your local press. Further advice on setting up a group can be obtained from the Civic Trust, whose address is given below.

Local authorities have a constitutional obligation to take notice of the views of local amenity societies. Letters from individuals also carry weight in a situation where the means of finding out local opinion are often severely limited. Letters to MPs and to the Department of the Environment also constitute evidence of public opinion which cannot be ignored. Remember also that an individual or a group can write to—or even telephone—the Department of the Environment (address and telephone number below) asking for a threatened building of value to be Listed immediately. Particularly where the Lists have not recently been updated, but not just in these cases, this is a most effective and readily available weapon. Enclose a photograph of the buildings concerned wherever possible when writing.

A group can often persuade the local authority to notify it of all planning applications, or of applications for Listed Building Consent or that affect Conservation Areas; these also have to be advertised in the local press. (The List can be inspected at the Town Hall or obtained from the Department of the Environment.) It can then make its comments and influence decisions on important cases. It can often also nominate a member to the Council's Conservation Area Advisory Committee, which local authorities are urged by the government to set up. Beyond this, it can press home to the Council its statutory responsibilities for conservation and get it to issue Repairs Notices, look after its own buildings, designate Conservation Areas and put in hand programmes of improvement in these Areas; and it can encourage the Council by doing some of its work for it and making detailed analyses of potential Areas for designation. The group can also have a vital impact by assembling the case for conservation and rehabilitation, in terms of economics as well as of aesthetics, in the face of developers' propaganda for demolition or a local council's blind commitment to comprehensive redevelopment in housing or the provision of shopping facilities. This may often involve pointing out what grants are available for conservation (information which can be obtained from the national societies) or finding a potential owner or developer (perhaps a housing association) that would be prepared to carry out rehabilitation. It can stimulate interest in local conservation issues by cultivating contacts with the local press. In extreme cases, it can organise petitions, and its principal effort may have to be directed at national government. As we said at the beginning, the group also has an important role in bringing local threats to the notice of the national societies (again photographs are helpful).

The principal amenity societies are as follows:

THE SOCIETY FOR THE PROTECTION OF ANCIENT BUILDINGS, 55 Great Ormond Street, London WC1N 3JA. (The father of the amenity societies, founded by William Morris. Principally concerned with pre-Georgian buildings, but gives technical advice on the repair of buildings of all dates.)

THE GEORGIAN GROUP, 2 Chester Street, London SW1X 7BB.

THE VICTORIAN SOCIETY, 1 Priory Gardens, Bedford Park, London W.4.

THE ANCIENT MONUMENTS SOCIETY, 33 Ladbroke Square, London W11 3NB. (In fact concerned with good buildings of all periods.)

The following national organisations can also give valuable assistance and support:

THE CIVIC TRUST, 17 Carlton House Terrace, London SW1Y 5AW. (Particularly concerned with townscape and Conservation Areas. Keeps a register of local amenity societies and gives them advice.)

THE TOWN AND COUNTRY PLANNING ASSOCIATION, 17 Carlton House Terrace, London SW1Y 5AS. (Operates a planning aid service for local groups.)

THE COUNCIL FOR THE PROTECTION OF RURAL ENGLAND, 4 Hobart Place, London SW1W 0HY. (Concerned with towns and villages as well as with the countryside. Has a wide network of branch organisations.)

THE ASSOCIATION FOR INDUSTRIAL ARCHAEOLOGY, Church Hill, Ironbridge, Telford, Salop TF8 7RE.

THE COUNCIL FOR BRITISH ARCHAEOLOGY, 8 St Andrew's Place, Regent's Park, London NW1 4LB. (Also concerned with buildings and monuments of the Industrial Revolution and other above-ground aspects of archaeology: it drew up the list of historic towns mentioned in the Introduction.)

THE FRIENDS OF FRIENDLESS CHURCHES, 12 Edwardes Square, London W8 6HG.

The relevant addresses of the DEPARTMENT OF THE ENVIRONMENT are 25 Savile Row, London W1X 1AB (telephone 734-6010) for Listing matters and the photographic library kept by the National Monuments Record, and 2 Marsham Street, London SW1P 3EB for senior staff. Its equivalents outside England are:

THE SCOTTISH DEVELOPMENT DEPARTMENT, St Andrew's House, Edinburgh EH1 3DD (telephone 031 556 8501).

THE WELSH OFFICE, Cathay's Park, Cardiff CF1 3NQ (telephone 0222 28066).

DEPARTMENT OF THE ENVIRONMENT, GOVERNMENT OF NORTHERN IRELAND, Parliament Buildings, Stormont, Belfast BT4 3SS (telephone 0232 63210).

The Civic Trust's *Environmental Directory* provides a very full list of all organisations, national and regional, of interest to those concerned with amenity and environment, price 60p post free.

Finally, we append a note on some helpful further reading. *Goodbye London* by Christopher Booker and Candida Lycett Green (Fontana, 1973) is a catalogue of development proposals threatening buildings and familiar streetscape throughout London, constituting challenges to action that have still to be taken up for the most part. *How to Run a Pressure Group* by Christopher Hall (Dent, 1974, £1.25) is an excellent practical guide. *The New Citizen's Guide to Town and Country Planning* by John Ardill (Town and Country Planning Association/Charles Knight, 1974, £1.25) is a guide to legislation and possibilities of action. The reports of the Dobry committee (*Interim* and *Final Report of the Committee to Review the Development Control System; Control of Demolition;* all from HMSO) make up-to-date reading and provide a stimulating approach to the complicated workings of the planning processes. *Preservation* by Wayland Kennet (Maurice Temple Smith, 1972, £2.40) is a most readable account of the rise of the conservation movement. The Victorian Society *Annual* each year, as well as giving interesting information on the cases the Society is involved with, provides valuable comment and criticism on the progress of the conservation battle. The journals of the Architectural Press (9-13 Queen Anne's Gate, London S.W.1., from your newsagent), the *Architectural Review* (monthly; 60p, £7.25 for a year) and the *Architect's Journal* (weekly; 20p, £10.50 for a year), are full of news and informed articles on conservation, making up for the often scanty and half-hearted treatment of conservation issues in the national press.